THE CITY OF

KT-461-010

E

DEVISED AND COLLABORATIVE THEATRE

Edited by Tina Bicât and Chris Baldwin

The Crowood Press

First published in 2002 by
The Crowood Press Ltd
Ramsbury, Marlborough
Wiltshire SN8 2HR

This impression 2018

City of Liverpool College

Acc No.   Date Cat

65825596   04·02·19

D.xc   RFID

712.028   £ 16·99.

BIC

Foreword © Clive Barker 2002
Introduction and Endnote © Tina Bicât and Chris Baldwin 2002
Chapter 1 © Chris Baldwin 2002
Chapter 2 © Haibo Yu 2002
Chapter 3 © Sabina Netherclift 2002
Chapter 4 © Bernd Keßler 2002
Chapter 5 © Paul Barker 2002
Chapter 6 © Ruth Naylor-Smith 2002
Chapter 7 © Tina Bicât 2002
Chapter 8 © Alison King 2002
Chapter 9 © Charlotte Cunningham 2002

All rights reserved. No part of this publication may be reproduced or transmitted in any form or by any means, electronic or mechanical, including photocopy, recording, or any information storage and retrieval system, without permission in writing from the publishers.

British Library Cataloguing-in-Publication Data
A catalogue record for this book is available from the British Library.

ISBN 978 1 86126 524 1

Photograph previous page: Devised work relies on the ideas and chance discoveries that occur in rehearsal.

Throughout this book 'he', 'his' and 'him' have been used as neutral pronouns and as such refer equally to males and females.

Line drawings by Annette Findlay

Typeset by Jean Cussons Typesetting, Diss, Norfolk

Printed and bound in India by Replika Press Pvt. Ltd.

CONTENTS

FOREWORD

Like many other forms of performance, devised theatre sneaked up on us. Endless volumes can be, and have been, devoted to the possible origins of melodrama, the musical, vaudeville. In a sense, devised theatre has always been there, and we could more easily try to establish at what point the producer took on the power of executive, the playwright rose to eminence as proprietary rights were established in the text, and the director was brought in to protect the financial interests of the backers. What has changed, over the last forty years or so, has been a fluctuating activity intending to draw into the creative process all the various talents of those members of the theatre ensemble, who have been disenfranchised by the concentration of power of decision in the hands of a few key members. The principle behind this has been that the now-established pattern of theatre, where a director instructs a team of actors in how to interpret the script of the playwright, has been strong on control and wasteful on imagination. The main alternative has been to find some way of working in which the imaginative potential of each of the members of the ensemble can be utilized to enrich the performance. It would not be stretching things too far to see this process as attempting to supplant oligarchic, or even dictatorial, control by a more democratic way of working. To ensure this requires some way of working that is capable of orchestrating the efforts of the ensemble, so that they work to harmonize the various tensions, and utilize the differing, and often conflicting, contributions into a rich dialectic, rather than a monofocal, blinkered vision. Devised and Collaborative Theatre brings together a group of theatre practitioners from all the fields, with a wealth of experience, to suggest ways in which this co-ordination can be brought about. In keeping with the spirit of the work itself, this is not an instruction manual for creating theatre, but a rich combination of experiences, ideas and practical suggestions, from which to draw in creating your own projects and productions.

PROFESSOR CLIVE BARKER

INTRODUCTION: COLLABORATIVE INVENTION
Chris Baldwin and Tina Bicât

Work begins on a scripted play or a piece of theatre: the director and producer choose their company and a copy of the script drops through their letterboxes; directors, technicians, designers and actors, in their offices and kitchens, read the words. Of course they will not all understand them in the same way. They will look at the ideas from the different viewpoints demanded by their particular job, but they will all read the same story, the same dialogue and the same stage directions. When they meet for the first time, they will have a baseline of common knowledge of the script to use as a jumping-off point.

In a devised project this baseline does not exist – or rather it does exist, but at the beginning of the process, only in the random imaginations of each company member. The line moves about – it will not stay in one place. The ideas of the company conspire to shift it as soon as it appears to have settled. And yet it is the very existence of this shifting path that makes devised work so demanding, risky and exciting. As the devising process develops, this path must settle and aspire to some kind of aesthetic coherence.

Devising makes particular demands upon those involved. Each member of the company must listen and talk to the others with trust and attention, in order to minimize the risk

that someone, and it may be the audience, will not have a blind idea of what is going on, and feel excluded. At the outset of a devising project there may be no definite story line or even a set cast list. The company must work in a way that is different from more conventional theatre practice, if such a thing exists – and this means everyone, and not just the actors and director. Everybody involved in a devising project needs not only to be conscious of their artistic brief and responsibilities, but also sensitive to the dynamics of intense collaborative group work.

How does the instigator of the work enthuse the company with their idea? How does a set-designer design without knowing where the play is set? How can music and movement be created when the emotions they express have yet to be presented? How can a costume be designed and cut for a character as yet unnamed? How does the director rehearse the actors, cast the play and plan the work schedule? What does the stage manager do without script or prop list? Where and when does the writer come in? And what on earth does the producer do about raising money, budget and publicity? All these questions and more are addressed in this book. The answers may not reflect your own particular needs or style of theatre practice, but the questions are ones that you are likely to address should you

A Note On the Text

There are few, if any, rules for this sort of work. The size and financial situation of the company makes each project different, along with the fact that devised work is often developed for a specific audience. Despite this, most chapters include check-lists, which may prove useful to someone who is doing the job for the first time. After a little experience you will create your own version of these lists, which will suit the way you work. This book has been written by experienced professional devising practitioners, who also, on occasion, teach their craft. Relevant exercises are included at the end of chapters where their respective authors think they would be useful to the reader. He and she are used throughout the book in an arbitrary manner as, of course, both sexes work in all departments of a theatre company. Suggestions for further reading on each discipline are included at the end of the book.

work in collaborative theatre. Devising projects can involve an army of makers or just involve two clowns in a rehearsal room for weeks on end. Whatever the context the questions remain roughly the same.

In a script-led production, the whole team has a common starting point: the director has probably chosen or even commissioned the play, and he might well have a clear line or conceptual starting point in mind early on in the process.

If the play is Shakespeare's *The Tempest*, perhaps the director wishes to focus upon the role of magic in the play – magic as an enabling force, magic as a demented, manipulative force, magic as liberation for the imagination, magic as a means of penetrating the Elizabethan mind. Such a guide, while still sketchy, gives the rest of the team plenty with which to begin work. Combining this conceptual starting point with the fact that the play is so well known, will help the producer begin to raise money and sell performances. The set and costume designers, the composer and movement director will also begin to discuss and experiment in order to find how best to focus audience attention on the visual, aural and movement-based notions of the magic in *The Tempest*. The director will usually work with the whole team and often use their discoveries to refine and develop his own work, both before rehearsals begin and during rehearsals.

The producer, writers of words and music, the director, designers and technical supporters will meet to begin creating the timing of the project, to assess the budget and its division, and to choose or explore the venue and its technical strengths and weaknesses. Many questions are addressed, though they cannot be answered conclusively. The most vital issue discussed is the construction of the company. How many actors? Male or female? Does the project need a movement director? Musicians? A puppeteer? Specialist advice on projection or pyrotechnics? All will use the discoveries from these discussions to define and develop their work. During rehearsals many more discoveries will be made, which will make the most exciting combinations of the use of space, sound and actors.

However, in a devising process the starting point is not necessarily, indeed not usually, a script. The seed of a devised piece always sprouts its first root in one imagination, and it is usually, though not invariably, the director's. Often the company who work together regularly are so familiar with each other's creative process that no one really knows where the idea starts. Nevertheless many of the same rehearsal stages must be passed through as in any other theatre production. The sequence of decision-making, and the discoveries that are made in rehearsal, can lead to unexpected outcomes in performance. As a result, the idea of devising has become one to which many more companies and audiences have become attracted. And what is more, as the traditional role of a text-based director has shifted from one of interpreter to one of conceptualist, aspects of devising work have crept into conventional theatre practice, if, as we say elsewhere, such a thing exists.

Devised work depends upon, and utilizes, the ideas and chance discoveries that occur in rehearsal more than does script-based work. This may be a contentious idea but the chapters in this book seem to prove the point. The prolific imaginations of the company, if well managed and focused, can be transformed from chaos into rich, elegant and often deeply resonant productions and performances for an audience. Yet despite the freedom of thought and action apparent in rehearsals of devised work, the project needs a leader with a firm grasp of the direction in which the work is heading. The inexperienced devising team will often waste valuable hours talking and arguing and, at the end of the rehearsal day, have little or no embryonic scenes or theatre to show for all their hard work. Mistakenly, in such cases, everyone sees themselves as a director, attempting to convince resentful others to follow their ideas. It is the role of the director to guide and inspire, to focus and nurse the project through rehearsals and, where humanly possible, to learn to predict when a certain alley may be a blind one. For

this reason, the book begins with a chapter on this pivotal role.

This book, therefore, has a very concrete aim. Rather than focusing on the fashionable and contemporary issues regarding devising, it aims to help students, and anyone new to devised theatre, to solve the technical problems that occur when starting work without a clear idea of the finished product. It will help to balance the exciting, creative drive of the work with the practical necessities of budget and the technical necessities of the production. Each chapter, while examining the unique responsibilities of a given role, also points to the stages a deviser must move through in order to get the thing finished and in front of an audience on time and within budget. Clearly, the picture of the devising process is not a complete one, but these chapters should assist in considering the stages a devising team will need to pass through, and the kinds of questions that need to be posed. 'He' and 'she' are used in an arbitrary manner in the text as, of course, both sexes do all jobs in the theatre.

In the spider diagram overleaf the box marked 'Starting point' contains a simple six-line story – a proposal for a scene, which might, in turn, become a show. This proposal was sent to each contributor to this book with a request to return it with the questions they would want answered as they started work on the project. The surrounding boxes record their immediate responses. This diagram offers a valuable insight into the way that people with differing responsibilities ask vitally different questions.

The costume designer asked:

- Do the audience react to the man with fear, affection, laughter or what?
- How old is the man and what does he do when he is not fishing?
- What is the set like? What era? What sort of weather?
- How can I help tell the story?

The actor asked:

- What do I know about the character?
- How old is he, how strong, how confident, is he depressed, i.e. what is his story?
- What style will the scene be played in? Naturalistic? With puppets? In mime or with props?

THE STARTING POINT: THE STORY

A man sits on a riverbank holding a fishing rod. The fishing line is extended into the water. All is still and calm. The fisherman stares at the water. Suddenly, the line jerks. A fish has been hooked! A huge struggle between fisherman and the fish commences.

The director asked:

- What will interest an audience? Where is the moral conflict?
- How do I represent the scene? Consult designers?
- Where is the surprise in the story? Work with writer, movement director and actors and improvise.

The writer asked:

- Where is the surprise in the story?
- How can I build in further turning points?
- Who are my principal and secondary characters?
- What happens, moment by moment?

The producer asked:

- What is going to be the hook for the audience? Is this scene based on an existing story or a recognizable character?
- How big a cast is this going to need?
- What other types of creative collaborators are essential?
- What is the style of the piece going to be, e.g. abstract or naturalistic?

The stage manager asked:

- Are you going to have a real fish/water?
- What, if any, environment/safety problems are there?
- What sort of fish is needed? What breed? Real or not?
- Where is this coming in the action?
- Will the audience see the struggle?
- Can we create this with lighting and sound and set?
- How much budget do we have?

The composer asked:

- Does the scene have dialogue or does the music carry the drama forward?
- What is the journey: from what state to what other state, and what obstacles are in the way?
- How long is each part?
- What is the budget for live musicians?
- Does the fisherman play a mouth-organ while he is waiting? Or a trumpet?
- What is the relationship with this scene to the whole play?
- How long have I got to write it?

The movement director asked:

- What does the director want from the scene: comedy, tragedy, the epic struggle?
- What is the action (or inaction) of the scene and how can we make it dynamic, rhythmic, visual and truthful?
- Who are the characters (fisherman and fish), how do they move and what is their physical relationship?

The set designer asked:

- What is the environment for the story?
- What are the physical requirements for the set?
- How big the budget is?
- What does the venue look like?
- When is the deadline?

1 THE DIRECTOR
Chris Baldwin

The director is one of the key figures in any theatre production but especially so in devised theatre. When a company begins to plan a devised production it is the director, over and above anyone else, who must have a clear picture of what needs to happen on the creative front at specific moments in the process. This chapter, therefore, describes the devising process from the director's point of view. We will begin by looking at the very early stages of a devising project, what might be called looking for the concept or underlying idea for the show. Though the chapter we will examine some of the more concrete things that actually need to happen in the rehearsal room in order to be ready for the first night.

THE ROLE OF THE DIRECTOR

Above all else the director is responsible for ensuring that the production is conceptually and aesthetically coherent, that the story is clearly told, that it can be seen and heard by the audience, that it is stimulating and

Director discussing an early idea with the group. Photo: Tina Bicât

entertaining, and, most importantly, that it is not boring! But to get to this point there are a number of specific tasks that must be set and completed, and a number of questions that must be posed and answered.

For the sake of clarity let us assume that it is the director who has had an idea for a devised show. The director must be convinced that the idea is a good one, that it contains the seeds for a really good piece of drama – something that will surprise, delight and, sometimes, shock the audience too. But what else must it contain? How do stories for theatre differ from other kinds of stories? See Chapter 2, on writing in devised theatre, for some further thoughts.

How does a director ensure that the devised piece will develop coherently? Clearly there are no fail-safe answers to this question. However, it is the director to whom the rest will turn for guidance and that crucial lead when people get lost from time to time. It is the director's job to ensure that the group 'finds the nut' of the project, clarifies that central idea that will drive the project forward and enable everyone else to do their job. Rather than being at the top of a hierarchical structure, the director is at the centre of the rehearsal fulcrum, ensuring that everyone is working together and, at the same time, making sure that the project remains conceptually consistent and elegant. But it should also be pointed out that the director does not have the answers to difficult problems secretly stored away waiting to reveal themselves at the correct moment. It is the team (of which the director is one) who must work to find the answers to the problems they have set themselves. So what can a devising director bring to a project? What can he ensure occurs during the design of the project from this position at the centre of the fulcrum?

A good devising director is bound to ensure that a period of 'research and design' is built into the project. This will enable ideas to be tested out with performers and the production team, to allow for a period of reflection before launching into a full scale rehearsal process. Let us look at this period in a little more detail.

THE RESEARCH AND DESIGN PERIOD

Almost every chapter in this book contains a section on research and design, which is the essential foundation for all investigative group work. Research can take many forms: from researching in libraries and on the internet, to a movement director observing how a wolf moves around a cage in a zoo. Good quality primary research, and the way you utilize it in rehearsal, will help you make discoveries both about your theme and the aesthetic decisions you make.

Plan to spend a solid week or ten days with the complete team assembled well before rehearsals are due to begin – or even before you have finally agreed to take the show into rehearsal. This week could take place up to a year before rehearsals are scheduled. If this is not possible, it should take place at least a few months before rehearsals are due to begin. The objectives listed below must still occur somehow, in order to enable everyone to do their work in the necessary order. If a block of ten days is logistically impossible, then plan a series of days or weekends, but try to ensure that it is a part of the project distinct from the rehearsal period.

Objectives of a Research and Design Period

- To present the initial stimulus to the whole group and monitor the response.
- To discover the story on which the show will hang, but not necessarily have a script.
- To agree with the 'core team' the aesthetic style the show will probably take.

Checklist 1: The Research and Design Period

The inner core team (discussed later):
- the director
- the producer
- the playwright

- the designer (s)
- the composer
- the movement director.

The outer core team:
- production manager

- performers/actors/dancers/acrobats.

Equipment/materials/supplies:
- a bare large room, as neutral as possible
- tables and chairs
- large sheets of cheap paper and thick marker pens

- coffee and tea machines
- large bowls of fruit and bottles of water on the tables.

Concrete Stimuli for Devising
Examples of narrative starting points
- a painting in an art gallery
- newspaper stories
- a painting
- a novel or short story

- a diary
- an historical account of the day the First World War broke out.

Examples of non-narrative starting points:
- an abstract painting in an art gallery
- a series of costumes or hats from different time periods

- a series of objects (ropes, crates and poles)
- six jars each containing a different smell
- a large suitcase full of old photographs.

The Week's Timetable
Days 1 + 2
Present initial stimuli, visit locations and museums, talk to specialists on the subject. At the end of day 2 run a question-orientated review session. The director needs to clearly outline what he needs to get out of the week and also invite the team to define what they need to achieve too. Everything should be written down.

Days 3 + 4 + 5
Begin looking for the story on which the show will hang.

Days 6 + 7 + 8
The following will depend on the nature of the project:
- workshops run by designer (and director)
- workshops run by composer (and director)

- workshops run by choreographer (and director).

Day 9
Review session: likely questions:
- where have we got to?
- to be used according to what is discovered from the review session.

- what are the next steps?

Day 10
- designer/director-led session on potential locations for the project.
- director/producer-led session on the potential audience.

- To learn what kind of team will be required for the rest of the project.
- To discover as much as possible about a potential location for the show and the potential audience.

In order to achieve these objectives, the director needs to keep a number of balls in the air at the same time. But the most crucial point to remember is that it is not only the director who has questions to answer. The whole team, especially the core team, will have their own sets of crucial questions and the director must ensure that these get answered too! The simplest way of ensuring this is to build a regular series of 'question and review' periods into the whole process.

THE INNER CORE TEAM

It is essential that the inner core team are present from the beginning of the research and design period and that, where humanly possible, this team stays constant throughout the rest of the process. The inner core team needs to know what is going on, from moment to moment, and participate at a fundamental level in all the key decisions. While the outer core team is clearly essential, the director and producer need to reserve the right to change or alter this team before rehearsals proper begin, if that is what the show requires. If, for example, it becomes clear, as a result of the research and design period, that the performers must be able to sing and juggle, then perhaps this will mean looking for another performer or even a replacement. This is perfectly acceptable professional practice as long as no promises are made to the performers that they will be in the final show.

Whatever the initial stimulus for a show, the director looks to ensure that the idea has the power to arrest. He uses the first collision between company and potential devising material to ask the question, 'Is it likely that the interest (or lack of interest) shown here would be shared by an audience in the future?'. The director must not only ask himself, but the whole group, this question. But it is a question that can only be *posed* on day 1 of the research and design period. If the question could be answered on the same day, then there would be little point in working any longer. The point at which an answer to the question is sought depends on the intuition of the director, but it must be answered before a commitment is made to spending all that money on a full rehearsal and production.

The first job then is to find a concrete way of testing whether the chosen stimulus is attractive, can be understood and made intriguing to a group of people other than the director. First, the devising stimulus needs to be offered to the whole group. If it is a short story, then the group can read it out loud. If it is a painting in an art gallery, then the whole group needs to see it by going to the gallery together. Perhaps the director can organize a meeting between the team and the gallery's education officer, who will be able to talk about the painting and the life and times of the artist. If the stimulus for the devising is a suitcase full of old photographs, then the director, writer and designer also need to plan the first morning carefully. How will the team encounter the suitcase? Will they be encouraged to begin thinking immediately about potential stories and connections between the photographs? If so, these will need to be recorded for later use.

Once the stimulus has been presented, the director needs to begin to ask as many questions as possible, both of himself but, more importantly, to the group. What, if anything, do we find surprising about this stimulus or story? What strikes us as shocking, memorable, interesting? What don't we understand? And if there is more than one stimulus, questions need to include the following: Do they have common elements? Do they have things not in common? And the answers to these questions, however provisional and makeshift, must be recorded for all to refer to as the week progresses.

At this point, the devising director is doing three jobs at the same time. First, he is seeing whether the rest of the team shares his personal interest in the stimulus. If it does not, the idea probably needs to be abandoned as the stimulus is likely to be of little interest to an audience either. Second, he is also using the opportunity to allow the group to find out about what interests them as a group. This is crucial, as the main difference between theatre and most other art forms is the fact that it is a collectively experienced art form. The

individual can experience a poem, but theatre always involves two or more – the actor and the single member of the public – and therefore the stimulus needs to resonate widely. Third, the director is facilitating the whole week – making sure that people agree how the week should be structured and ensuring that everyone is asking the questions that needed to be answered.

During these early days it is best if the director keeps his points of view as private as possible. They are important, but not at this point; he can simply ask questions and ensure the process is recorded. In order to ensure that this is as collective and open as possible, he might come to the workshop with huge sheets or rolls of paper and pens. If the paper is fixed to the wall, all can see it, refer to it and write on it.

Making a record of decisions for rehearsal reference.
Photo: Fernando Bercebal

At the beginning of the week this paper can be used to record the objectives of the week (both collective and individual) and later used (perhaps on the last but one day) as a means of measuring the degree of success of the week. The paper on the wall is also used to record everything else that happens and everyone should be encouraged to write things down. As responses and ideas begin to emerge, the director can make sure that they get recorded by all and for all to see. Most importantly, the director is taking on the role of enabler – he is not telling the group why the stimulus is important, indeed the reverse. He is using a strategy every good teacher/enabler uses every day: he is asking open-ended questions and avoiding those kind of questions which have implicitly correct and incorrect answers.

Prompt Points

Who is responsible for developing the story in a devising context? The director? The playwright? The actors? The designer? Maybe all of these and others too. This chapter raises certain questions about structuring the theatrical story, but you will find much more in Chapter 4, Chapter 3 and Chapter 7 on how the actor can use props and costumes to tell stories.

Once a response to the initial stimulus has been gathered (and let's assume it is a positive one) the next two stages can begin: the quest for a theatrical story and theatrical form.

A story for theatre needs to be based on a series of playable actions. **Pinocho. Teatro Narea and Teatro Armar, Spain 2001. Director: Chris Baldwin.** *Photo: Javier Bercebal*

Example of Devising Action Synopsis: Scene 1 – *Bright Angel*

1961. The scene: an incomplete corrugated iron wall with a red line painted on the floor a metre away from the wall. An East German soldier enters and places his gun on the floor. He then takes a piece of corrugated iron from the floor and stands it between two other pieces of corrugated iron, thus completing a section of a wall. He picks up his gun and exits.

Enter Rudi and Sylvia, two young people aged 17. They hug and kiss and then begin to fool about.

The soldier re-enters, gun cocked, and arrests Rudi. Sylvia is left. Lights down.

*They hug and kiss and begin to fool about....*Bright Angel. *Proteus Theatre, UK, 1997.*
Directors: Chris Baldwin and Bernd Keßler. Photo: Jeremy Pakes

Theatre, at its core, is deeply interested in the way people relate to one another and live alongside one another (or must, do not, cannot or will not live alongside one another). The devising process is one in which the team must search out the stories that contain interesting or puzzling accounts of the way people interact with one another and then locate what we might describe as 'the playable actions'. Then we need to find entertaining ways of presenting these stories to our public. That is what much of this first week is about.

Locating the theatrical story is probably the most crucial element in any show building process and one that is explored in more depth elsewhere in this book. The key point to remember, from the director's point of view, is that whatever the final story (discovered, chosen or made up), it must be a story which is playable by performers.

A story for theatre needs to be based on a series of actions, which are presented in real time to an audience. Even an account of Galileo's discussions with the Roman Catholic Church in the seventeenth century will need to be presented in the present tense. In this first period of the project it is essential to locate a story as quickly as possible. Once this has been done, then the playwright, director and performers can construct an 'action synopsis', scene for scene, which can be used for more detailed devising in the next stage of rehearsals.

Once a story has emerged from the initial stimulus, then the team can begin looking for a form and style of presentation for their show. It is for this reason that it is essential that the writer, composer, movement director and designer(s) are in the workshops this week. If they have been involved in examining the initial stimulus and then finding the story on which the show rides, they will be able to offer very concrete suggestions at this point. Each member of the core team (except perhaps the producer) can be given a day with the whole team to present a workshop aimed at exploring the initial stimulus from their own perspective. The set designer might, for example, use this opportunity to present how three visual elements be used and transformed as the story progresses. The composer might use half a day with the performers to experiment with how the very same visual elements might be used as musical instruments. The movement director and costume designer might work with the whole team to explore how costume might be used by more than one performer as a way of sharing one role. (See Chapter 5 and Chapter 6 for more ideas on how to use time in research and design.)

The penultimate day of the research and design week needs to be left unplanned until the day arrives. Quite possibly the director will know what needs to happen, as things have been slow earlier in the week or the composer, for example, needs more time to complete a workshop. It is essential to begin the day with a review session to make sure that everybody gets a chance to say what he or she still needs to get from the week. Remember that the director must not only make sure he has the answers to the questions in his mind but also needs to enable others to find theirs. The day can then be structured in order to ensure needs are met as much as possible.

The final day of the week can be dedicated to thinking about a potential location for the show. Theatre does not need to be in a specially built theatre space. There are many potential theatre sites all around us from disused swimming pools to old warehouses, from school halls to prison cells. The issues surrounding access to such spaces and health and safety are complex but not insurmountable, and can pay enormous creative dividends. To watch a huge metal boat sink in front of your very eyes on a disused London dock may stick in the imagination of your audience for the rest of their lives!

The potential audience for the show is a critical consideration, as it will influence not just the content of the show but the resources available for the show. For example, while young people may make up over 30 per cent of our population, they certainly do not attract an equivalent amount of public or private money available to the arts organizations. Resources and money can be found from the oddest of sources and it is worth thinking collectively about where to find the money you need.

Finding the unified aesthetic style is an important element of success. Pinocho. *Teatro Narea and Teatro Armar, Spain 2001. Director: Chris Baldwin.*
Photo: Javier Bercebal

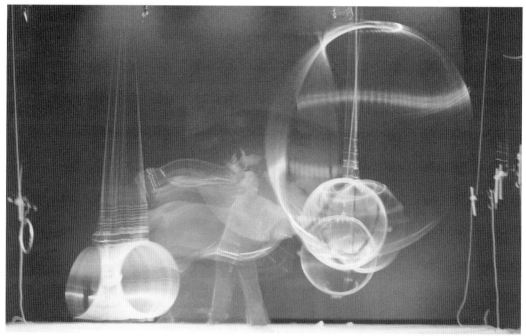

Various chapters in this book have sections entitled 'budgeting' – and the very fact that designers and stage managers, not just producers, discuss financial matters, indicates how fundamental money matters can be in devising.

If, by the end of the week, the director has gained a positive response to the initial stimulus, worked with the team to find a story on which to hang the show, knows what kind of performance team will be required next, and begun to locate a potential unified aesthetic style, then the week has been a stomping success!

All of this work can now be developed and extended in the weeks and months to come, by the individual artists and support teams who constitute the company, under the watchful eye of the director. By the time rehearsals begin, a number of concrete decisions will have been made.

THE PRE-REHEARSAL PERIOD

While the producer works with funders, marketing strategies and tour timetables, the director works with the designers, composer and movement director, and begins thinking about building a performance team.

The research and design period should have provided a huge number of ideas to all the inner core team members. They will now wish to use the pre-rehearsal period to do further research and come back to the director with firm propositions. While this is to be

---

Checklist 2: Pre-Rehearsal Period

- Plan weekly production meetings with the inner core team and the production manager.
- Complete action synopsis.
- Plan and run auditions workshop.

Workshop audition skills table

	Male/ Female	Playing Ages	Music Instrument 1–10	Singer 1–10	Dance 1–10	Juggle 1–10	Stage Fighting	Group Work Skills	Other Notes
Candidate 1									
Candidate 2									
Candidate 3									
Candidate 4									
Candidate 5									
Candidate 6									

encouraged wherever possible, it might also be that the research and design period must run directly into the rehearsal period. In such cases decisions are simply speeded up. Whether there is a gap or not, it is important to remember that the composers and designers can do very little until the story on which the show will hang has been agreed. If there is no gap between research and design and the rehearsal period then the story must be found first and quickly. Then the rest can get to work.

If the first period of workshops have ended with a clear need for actors who can play musical instruments and juggle, then auditions will need to be held to find these folk. Devising also requires other special skills from performers.

How much work can be done prior to rehearsals will always depend on the nature of the devising process. If a playwright uses the research and design period to generate ideas for a play and then writes a draft, much the same procedure for putting on a text-based production can occur. In devising it is more likely that a detailed synopsis of the story might be generated, and no more. In this case, the designers and other inner core team members will have plenty to get on with, but they will need constant access to the director. Weekly production meeting are times when this can occur. It is absolutely essential that the production manager is also at these meetings, as she or he will be responsible for pulling the whole show together from a technical point of view.

Auditions are probably best organized more as workshops in which everyone can participate to allow you and other core team

Working on detailed moments may take days while actors develop new skills. **Pinocho.** *Teatro Narea and Teatro Armar, Spain 2001. Director: Chris Baldwin.* Photo: Fernando Bercebal

members to get some insight into how the candidates work as team members. As a director looking for good devising actors, you are looking for skills over and beyond the performance ones. By designing a skills table beforehand you will not forget to look out for specific talents as the workshop progresses. And if you find someone who is fascinating, talented and keen to join the project do not be too afraid to change your plans. Plans are simply the servants of good intuition.

Checklist 3: Director's Questions

Script: Will the playwright be producing text each morning or during the day or not at all? Will the actors, playwright and director be doing this work together in rehearsal? If so, who will record the decisions?

Design: Is the set design ready? Can a model be presented to the whole team on day 1? If not, what and when will the designer need (a workshop with the company) in order to prepare her final ideas? Who is designing the lighting?

Costume: Are these going to be developed as characters emerge in rehearsal or prior to rehearsal? Or a bit of both? Devising allows for the former, by far a richer way of working. But if this is to occur the director needs to make sure that the costume-making team have enough time and resources to have their work ready on time.

Music and movement: What do the composer and movement director need? More workshops? Dedicated rehearsal time with the whole cast for 6 hours a week?

Stage management: Who is agreeing a working timetable with the director and producer? When is the cut-off date for asking for props? How and when will technical rehearsals take place?

Marketing: As the show moves towards the first night, what demands will be made of the director? Time out of rehearsals? What keys points need to be rehearsed? Should he be asked to talk about the show or the target audience? Where will clean clothes be kept for publicity appearances?

Producing: The director, producer, stage manager and union representatives from the company will need to agree the rehearsal timetable, hours overtime, and so on.

Working through the script during a pause in rehearsal.
Photo: Fernando Bercebal

THE REHEARSALS

Once the performance team is complete, audience chosen, story agreed and location found, the devising process can enter its final stage with the commencement of fully blown rehearsals.

The major job ahead is for the devising director to pull all the threads together into a unified and coherent whole. For the sake of clarity we will work on the basis of a four-week rehearsal process and now look briefly at some of the stages that a company must pass through during the month.

Using check list 3, it is possible to construct a pretty clear timetable for a month of rehearsals. Since there are so many variables, you will need to draw up your own timetable.

An example of a pre-planned timetable is shown below. In reality it will need to be visited daily and adapted where necessary:

Clearly the role of a director is hydra-like – looking in many directions at the same time

Week 1	
Monday	Company meets. Design elements presented. Synopsis or devising stimuli presented.
Tuesday	Group-building exercises – work begins on action synopsis.
Wednesday	Action synopsis.
Thursday	Action synopsis.
Friday	Action synopsis + design workshop – details agreed.
Saturday	Action synopsis + music rehearsal?
Week 2	
Monday	Production meeting. Action synopsis – scene by scene detailed rehearsal – character development.
Tuesday	Action synopsis – scene by scene detailed rehearsal – character development with costume designer present.
Wednesday	Action synopsis – scene by scene detailed rehearsal – character development. Music rehearsal.
Thursday	Action synopsis – scene by scene detailed rehearsal – character development with costume designer present.
Friday	Action synopsis – scene by scene detailed rehearsal – character development. Movement rehearsal.
Saturday	Half-day dedicated to music. Half-day dedicated to design.
Week 3	
Monday	Production meeting + first staggered run through with whole team present.
Tuesday	Rehearsal of 'bits'.
Wednesday	Rehearsal of 'bits' + rehearsal of 'bits'.
Thursday	Second staggered run through + rehearsal of 'bits'.
Friday	First uninterrupted run through.
Saturday	Second uninterrupted run through. Production meeting to conclude planning of technical week
Week 4	
Monday	Lighting and sound/music technical rehearsals.
Tuesday	Lighting and sound/music technical rehearsals.
Wednesday	Full dress rehearsal.
Thursday	Show opens.

A sample pre-planned timetable.

and listening to many, often competing, voices. However, apart from all the tasks the director must perform across the company, he must save his energy for the performance team. They will need to trust that he can help them form into an effective and creative team, learn to tell the story, learn about their characters, and be ready for that first night. Each morning rehearsals should therefore begin with at least an hour of carefully planned physical exercises designed to help the actors prepare their bodies for the day and to help them cohere as a group. There are many wonderful books and resources available to a director in relation to this.

While the performance team is at the centre of the director's attention, from this point forward he cannot afford to forget an invisible, yet crucial, ingredient in the recipe: the audience! Before weaving all the parts together, the devising director (with the playwright and performers) must work to ensure that the series of actions, which constitute the story, are constructed in such a way as to provoke, amuse and intrigue an audience. Week 1 of rehearsals is likely to be almost completely dedicated to getting the story 'up and running'. On day 1 of rehearsals, and after a warm up session, the director begins to use the action synopsis to look for the playable actions.

FIRST REHEARSAL: A DIRECTOR'S POINT OF VIEW

'Action One' of our devised show is of a man sitting on a river bank holding a fishing rod. An actor takes up this position. The fishing line is extended into the water. All is still and calm. The actor playing the man stares in to the water. The key question for a director and writer might be a surprising one: it is not what happens next but what the audience wants or expects to happen next. Our job, in a devising

context, is to explore this concrete question using theatrical means. The company predicts that the audience at this stage of the show will simply want something interesting to happen.

So the director suggests the following to the actor playing the fisherman: The fishing line suddenly jerks. A fish has been hooked. The expectation of the audience will thus rise: something is beginning to happen. A huge struggle between the fisherman and the fish commences and the bigger the better as far as the audience is concerned. Once the situation has been set up, then the audience will begin to ask a very specific question, a question the devising director and playwright must be able to predict; 'What ought to happen?'. Clearly there is not one single answer to this question, as it depends on the moral standpoint of each member of the audience. Some will want to see the fish escape, some will wish it to be caught, some will wish the fisherman to drown for causing the fish such misery! Once these opinions have been provoked by the action, we will now need to take the audience to the next level. The director is always asking, 'What does the audience need to see and know next?' – not as a way of simply keeping them happy but because the ability to use action on stage to create expectation in the mind of the public is at the core of all dramatic storytelling.

We need to show the audience what does happen next. The writer and director, and the actor in the improvization, decide that from within the basket on which the fisherman sits a mobile phone begins to ring. What does the fisherman do? Catch the fish or answer the phone? Another moral dilemma to be presented to the audience. He answers the phone while struggling to keep the rod taut. It is the fisherman's nine-year-old son. 'Dad, good morning' says the son, 'It's my birthday...and you promised to be here when I woke up!' Immediately the audience will have to review everything they have been thinking up to this point. The centre of the action has shifted from the battle between the fish and the fisherman to the son and the father. Consequently, the audience is forced to work harder, and as a result enjoy the process even more. This is a story that can be played in theatre as it is action-based and takes the audience through a series of questions: 'What is going to happen? What ought to happen? What does happen?'.

This series of questions must be predicted by the director/playwright/performer team and theatrical answers prepared in rehearsal. If this process is followed, step by step, using the action synopsis as a guiding tool, then a show will begin to emerge. As the action is made more and more clear, the designers, composers and stage managers can do their jobs more fully as explained in the following chapters.

If the first week of full-scale rehearsals is predominantly focused on action development, then towards the end of this week is a very good time to ask the composer, movement director and designers to be in rehearsal with the actor-performers as they will often have very exciting ideas, which will radically enrich the process. Week 2 can often be dedicated to detailed rehearsal of each scene in much the

During rehearsals groups of actors can work on different scenes at the same time.
Pinocho. *Teatro Narea and Teatro Armar, Spain 2001. Director: Chris Baldwin.*
Photo: Fernando Bercebal

Carefully selected props can allow other non-actor based characters to emerge. **Pinocho.** *Teatro Narea and Teatro Armar, Spain 2001. Director: Chris Baldwin.* Photo: Javier Bercebal

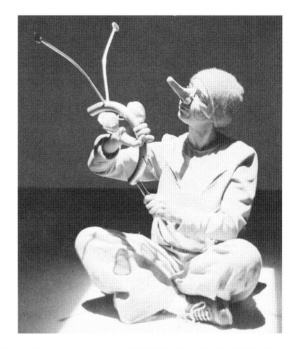

(Below) Designers, directors and actors co-operate to find powerful moments. **Pinocho.** *Teatro Narea and Teatro Armar, Spain 2001. Director: Chris Baldwin.* Photo: Javier Bercebal

same way as any other text-based rehearsal, as long as week 1 has generated concrete 'playable actions' for each scene. Week 3 will end in the first run of the piece – a very exciting and daunting moment, and in many respects will determine what needs to be done with the remaining time. In the last days of rehearsal, much of what a director can do is strictly limited by technical requirements. The production manager will be playing a significant role during these last few days, leaving the director to play a juggling game. Not only must the actors learn their technical role, but also keep their performances fresh, prepared and ready. Apart from helping the actors in this double task the director must work with the lighting designer, set and costume designers, and composer on all the outstanding technical considerations. With a good team around him, the director will discover that this role is not as impossible as it may at first seem. It only seems that way!

Technical rehearsals and the first-night needs are much the same as any other kind of show. Although it sounds like a contradiction, it is best if actors are given most of the day off on the day of the first show and only meet at the theatre or the space two or so hours before the show opens. Then the director knows that the actors can at least try to relax a little and he can concentrate on last minute technical or publicity needs – should there be any.

If the director oversees, co-ordinates and guides the rehearsal process, then he is at his most influential up to the first night. Indeed, after that the director can only really offer observations and comments to the actors and technical teams. Of course, the project may be constructed in such a way as to have a series of public viewings during the process. Whatever the project, the director must step back into the shadows on the first night and let the actors, music, design and, most importantly, the imagination of the audience do their jobs.

However, it can be that post-show changes are required because audience feedback tells the company that something is not understood or an idea might be more effective if made more simple. When such feedback is received, it is best not to become defensive (let alone aggressive) and instead, if time and resources allow, attempt to introduce such changes as precisely as possible.

FINDING THE 'PLAYABLE ACTIONS'

Here is a series of exercises, which will help you locate the skeleton of a dramatic story. It also encourages you to think about where the audience will be sitting when they see the story and how this might affect the decisions you make as a director.

Exercise 1: Identify the Important Events in the Story

This can be done by asking the group to boil their devising story down to half a sheet of paper. Then the group needs to divide the story into separate episodes and establish the turning points or the important events that carry the story a stage further. Once these have been located we can move onto the next stage.

Exercise 2: Make Still Images of the Key Moments in the Story

Divide the group into sub-groups if you can. If the group contains ten people, they could work in two groups. Then there is the potential for one group to act as an audience for the other. Each group is given an episode or two and asked to respond to the episodes by preparing a series of still images (or photos or sculptures) using their bodies to depict the key interesting, moments from their part of the story. They can respond by simply reconstructing a moment from the story itself or by responding symbolically or allegorically.

Finding the key moments through still images. Photo: Tina Bicât

When the images are presented to the other half of the team, do not allow the 'makers' to tell the rest what it is about. Rather ask those onlookers (the audience) to choose a position from which they like to view the image. Ask them, one by one to describe what they see. Try asking the following questions;

- Why have you chosen to view the image from this position?
- Where, for you, is the focal point? (Multi-focus? Inside? External?)
- Which character has the most status (power) in the image?
- Which character has the least status (power) in the image?

The answer to these questions must be listened to by the makers of the image very carefully, as they represent clues as to how a more formal audience might respond at a later date. They also give the makers valuable information about what to change in their image to elicit the response they were looking for. Move on to more open questions: what do they find intriguing, interesting, unable to fathom about the image they are looking at?

In this way we are hearing from an audience very early on in the process, and those who have made the image are hearing (straight from the horse's mouth) ideas on how to improve, change and develop their potential story. Repeat the process for the other group(s) and then send the groups back into rehearsal to alter, change, abandon, develop their images. Do not, as a director, intervene in these groups. Let them work alone if at all possible. Then you will be as surprised as an audience when you see the end product! Make sure everyone is involved if at all possible – not just actors but designers too. After an hour or two of generating theatrical vignettes in this fashion, the director, playwright and the team will need to reflect collectively, discuss their findings and the nature of their work, and work out what to do next. The next stage will probably require research: collecting more stories, accounts, specialist points of view, telephone calls, time in libraries or on the web.

29

2   SET DESIGN
Haibo Yu

Designing for a play without a script can challenge the most experienced designers. The well-established and traditional method of theatre production has always taken the form of the 'Page to Stage' concept, where the designer takes all the necessary information from the script before deciding the direction of research and initiating the design process. When designing for a devised theatre piece, where no script exists, it is often difficult to anticipate what is required in terms of location, scene changes, props, etc. before rehearsals commence.

The irony is that as the shape of the piece becomes progressively clear, the designer is left with less time for set/props construction. Even worse, constant changes to the set/prop list suggested by the continuous improvisation

Three corrugated rusty metal sheets and barbed wire represent the Berlin Wall and afterwards are transformed into other locations. **Bright Angel. Proteus Theatre, UK 1997. Directors: Chris Baldwin and Bernd Keßler.** *Photo: Haibo Yu*

	Design for Scripted Theatre	Design for Devised Theatre
Designer's role	Designer	Visual adviser, co-director and designer
Order of design progress	Designer–rehearsal	Rehearsal–design
Requirement for design completion	Design is completed and fixed after the production meeting	Continuous design development and alteration during the rehearsal process
Use of space	Actors' movement is affected by the space provided in advance	Space is designed according to the scene blocking
Major scenery element	Comprehensive combination of set and props	Actors and props, especially action props, neutral set such as levels and blocks
Principle design media	Scaled colour model and technical drawings	Sketch and rough model
Set construction period	Relatively long	Very short
Budget	Various	Usually very low

Design tasks.

may mean that the complete list for the design department may not be ready before the final rehearsal. Since the designer cannot afford to wait for this check list to arrive, it is important to take some design action from day one, or at least make some advance preparations for this clouded design task.

Although the uncertain nature of devised theatre may confuse and worry designers, it can give them a commitment to the project far beyond their usual confines, and a particular joy and involvement in overcoming the constant challenges.

THE DESIGNER'S ROLE WITHIN DEVISING

The design process for devised theatre uses a different approach to that for normal theatre design practice (see the comparison chart above). Designing without a script demands the foresight to predict the

Prompt Points

If you have read Chapters 5, 8 and 9, you might have noted that almost everybody suggests that the sequence in which decisions are made is different in devised theatre to text-based theatre. This important point needs serious discussion by any company new to devising.

forthcoming design. Both designer and design must retain the flexibility to cope with continuous changes during the entire rehearsal period.

The designer's responsibility in relation to the company often goes far beyond the boundaries of more commonplace set design. In the early phase of production planning, the designer's involvement with the director, producers or the writer is essential. The designer's vision of the future production, and his expertise in technical theatre, will influence the aesthetic concept and visual style of the performance. Design ideas put forward at this stage can enrich the director's concept and a designer's wild imagination can inspire the playwright. Wide knowledge of various design concepts and skills will prove most important in the search for the most suitable visual style and for economical technical interpretation.

The designer is expected to attend some rehearsals, and for this an understanding of all related disciplines in the theatre is essential. The designer may work directly with the actors to transpose the design ideas (e.g. different levels on the stage or the use of a large sheet of fabric) into actions, and acquire from them the instant feed-back that will lead to workable improvements and modifications.

REVERSING THE PROCESS

The working order of the design process seems completely chaotic when assembling ideas for devised theatre. Unlike the more familiar process, the starting point is most likely to be a chat with the director. There may be experimental improvisations in a rehearsal room. Since there is no script or pre-set boundaries at this early stage to limit the company's creative imaginations, the key creators (the director,

Set for a Greek play. The broken pottery image with levels provides a strong geographic vision and a flexible acting space for a devised physical theatre piece.
Photo: Haibo Yu

set designer, costume designer, movement director, etc.) are able to launch a series of free discussions. Through these they can settle the theme and draw a rough guideline for each department, to co-ordinate the overall style. The budget distribution may also be discussed.

The most significant point about designing for devised theatre is that the designer sets up a loose framework of scattered ideas, rather than a finished design project; then, with a completely open mind, he presents this to the actors. It is essential for the designer to observe the devising in progress, and to be able to respond quickly to any problems which surface during the rehearsal sessions. Design ideas, particularly the manipulation of space, can only be finalized after having been tested in the rehearsal room, refined by the designer and approved by the director.

SIMPLIFIED DESIGN

A humble budget forces the designer to be economical and efficient; it will have a vital effect on the scale, as well as the style, of the design. For this reason, a designer's first question when he takes the job will be to ask how much he can spend. When the budget is small, everything that appears on stage has to be highly selective. If the job can be done with two chairs, then never think about having third one. Minimalism and simplicity should be seriously considered as valuable design principles for low-budget theatre productions. Priority should be given to objects that are significant to the acting, e.g. objects that have direct physical contact with the actors. Any ambitious attempts that create magnificent illusions but fail to focus on the acting itself should be avoided, or at least viewed with great

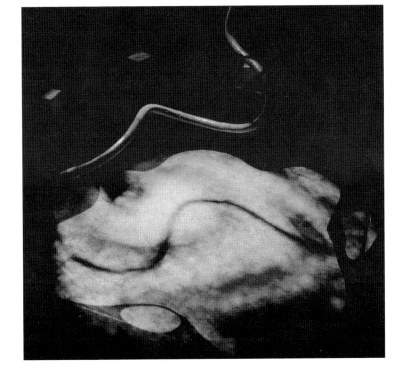

Binding Flesh, *devised by Drama Department St Mary's University College. The image of the acting space is a human body, which is simplified as a painted womb on the floor and blood vessels hanging above the stage.*
Photo: Haibo Yu

caution. There is no money to waste on mere decoration.

ECONOMICAL REALIZATION

When working under financial pressure, the construction, planning and building techniques for the set/props are as important as the design itself. The use of different materials and craft skills can make a huge difference to the cost. Hardboard is cheaper than plywood; metal texture on plastic sheets is much less costly than real metal; economical fabrics can be substituted for expensive cloth like velvet and can be disguised to have the same visual effect from a distance. Familiarity with a wide range of materials is vital and the ability to hunt for, find and cost them grows with experience.

Very few devising companies will have their own scenic workshop or will be able to afford to hire a professional scenic company to build the set. They sometimes even find it difficult to bring enough technicians on board. In most circumstances the designer and production management team become the painters, carpenters or electricians. In a student production, human resource is never a problem but close supervision of technical quality, and particularly safety, must be planned properly.

Adaptation from Jane Eyre *and other works. On the spiral-shaped mirrored floor the actors change costume and props on the stage. The costume rails are displayed as part of the set throughout the performance. Photo: Haibo Yu*

INITIAL DISCUSSIONS

Initial discussion between creators, in the early stages of production, forms the fundamental structure of the work to be devised. Artistic and technical issues are covered in these sessions; an outline of the scenario can be shaped despite the fact that nothing precise can be decided at this moment. Agreements with other artists over the visual forms and style are of great importance. With these in place, designers can work along the now clarified design guidelines. They can keep in step with other departments without worrying that their styles might have drifted apart. This will ensure that the flexible design process is constantly under control.

Devised theatre needs more collaboration than scripted theatre as many more group decisions have to be made. It is difficult to lay down a precise task list for a designer to follow in the pre-production period. However there are some steps common to all such work that need to be taken while working with a devising team.

SOURCE MATERIALS

The motivation to make a devised theatre piece can be sparked by anything: a piece of news on the paper's front page, a hot social issue, a friend of a friend's private story or just a natural scene. These catalysts can have a

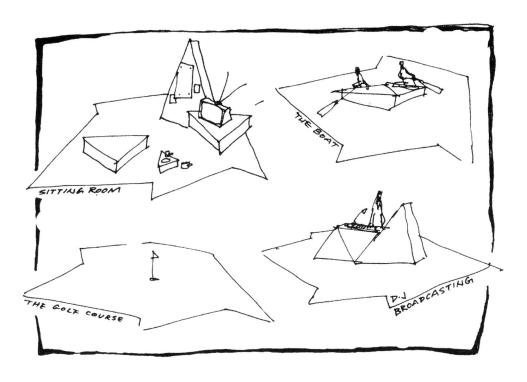

A pre-rehearsal drawing for Whale. *Harrogate Theatre, 1998. Director: Chris Baldwin. Shows how the set parameters – triangles – are to be used in different scenes.* Photo: Haibo Yu

BOOKS.

Using wooden panels to represent the books – a highly theatrical invention which was inspired by the temporary props used during rehearsal. **Don Quixote.** *Proteus* **Theatre, 1997. Director: Chris Baldwin.** *Photo: Haibo Yu*

complete story line or be just a few broken images.

Most devised theatre work is about events happening around us or about historical topics that relate to our society. It is rare to see a piece that is set against a period backdrop and not influenced by today's material or spiritual reality.

The designer should be able to judge what is the most valuable information for his future design from the primary sources of inspiration. The very first raw material, which inspired the devising ideas, can have occurred in various forms: in writing, in pictures or from objects or observations of life. The director and his collaborators, in the series of initial discussions, have to decide the part of the material that is transferable from its original

form to a stage performance. These discussions are sometimes fruitful but sometimes lead to long and fruitless debate. The designer, as one of the participants of these discussions, should always take particular interest in any visual material presented in the early discussions. Visual inspiration strikes immediate sparks in the designer's imagination.

TECHNICAL PRACTICALITIES

The original inspiration for a devised piece can be driven by visual motivation. However the technical practicality of using this visual image needs to be confirmed in the very early stages of the preparation period. Designers often find themselves in the position of theatre consultants and are asked to answer technical questions outside their design role. A wide range of knowledge and experience in technical theatre is necessary to answer these queries. They must also be capable of making creative and practical suggestions, which will enable the production to be more visually exciting.

Often queries about special requirements will come up before the first meeting: Can we hang the actors in the air? Can they move freely when wearing the harness that will enable them to fly? How practical is it to convert the existing auditorium into an open studio space? Performing arts have evolved to include complicated multimedia effects; from the conventional play to contemporary physical theatre, from traditional scenic techniques to industrial-standard set construction, from ordinary spotlight to pre-programmed digital projection. Today's theatre can make anything happen on stage. Helicopters can hover above the actors and witches can fly over the audience. It is hard for theatre-makers today to ignore the technical miracles available to them. They are keen, budget permitting, to employ these new techniques, to enrich their theatrical ideas. The team, and particularly the director, tend to seek technical answers from the designer. It is also the designer's job to invent and produce both magnificent theatrical effects and simple, low cost tricks.

RESEARCH

In-depth research is essential for finding the most suitable production shape and the metaphors to visualize the performance. This is usually a time-consuming and unpredictable task. If the designer is lucky he might accidentally come across exactly what he is looking for. Unfortunately this rarely happens. Research is so important that no designer, however experienced, can assume they have enough stored knowledge for a new project. Serious research will always produce further evidence and deeper understanding.

The range of research is so wide that, though libraries, museums and observations from life are still the principal resources, anything around us could provide valuable information. The choice of form is wide too: material in print, on tapes, observations, interviews, and so on. To avoid wasting time on blind searching, a research target and loose areas for study should be set, perhaps divided into several categories such as general background, visual images and observation from life. They may than be subdivided yet further, perhaps historically or geographically.

Background research is the same broad task as general research in other fields: it helps the designer to an intimate knowledge of the related area; it is the first step of the whole design process; and its form can be totally different according to the topic concerned and is not, at this stage, precise. Later, the designer will need to make a more detailed study. Another media, such as a novel, a film, a video or a piece of music, might inspire the devising work. The original source of this work and any critical reviews or analytical studies must be added to the research list.

Visual image research is the most crucial stage for the design project. All the information the designer collects during this period can be evidence for the visual detail of the production, and exciting new ideas are often generated at this time. The ideal source of first-hand images for a modern topic is observation of real life and, for an historical theme, museums and art galleries. When these are not available or appropriate, designers hunt images in book illustrations, art galleries and libraries. For other ideas for performance related research see Chapters 3, 6 and 7.

In order to locate the required books with ease, and to know where to start looking, it is

Weathered Arm, *devised from the original work by Thomas Hardy. Six wooden panels transform the acting space into houses, a stable, the church, a country path and a market, and so on. Photo: Haibo Yu*

essential to become familiar with how the books are arranged in a library. Consult the computer catalogues and use a search engine to locate books where the needed images are most likely to be found. Another practical tip when hunting for images in a particular section, is to skim all books that attract your eye, rather than choosing books by their titles.

Generally speaking the historical and geographical information so frequently needed for reference by designers can be found in the related subjects (history and geography).

These are normally arranged by countries and regions but may be found in the travel section. Special images may be found under specific subjects, e.g. farmer's tools in the agriculture section or a rose window in the architecture section.

TENTATIVE IDEAS

Scattered design ideas will spring to the designer's mind as soon as the research is under way. A good image can create an immediate response in the designer and may trigger off a series of imaginative visions.

However, the very first ideas, in most cases, are tentative and may be overturned by the images the designer comes across a few minutes later. On some occasions, these rejected ideas may return after several rounds of consideration. It is hard to predict how this complicated thought process will develop. It is wise to keep a clear record of the non-linear design development by keeping a designer's logbook. Every important turning point for new ideas should be clearly reflected in this record. Some may be replaced by better and stronger images, while others may be rejected due to impracticality.

Theoretically, there cannot be pre-determined designs for devised theatre. But the actors cannot start their experimental rehearsals with nothing but their bodies to help them, and the designer has to set a deadline to provide them with a few ideas of the set.

SPACE MANIPULATION

The primary goal of theatre design is to combine providing physical acting spaces with creating the visual form of the performance. These criteria are always the same, whether for opera, dance, plays without scripts or any other branch of the performing arts. A flexible acting space, which can be smoothly manipulated and transformed into the required physical locations, is particularly necessary when devising theatre.

A neutral construction with levels served as the basic set for several different productions during a performance season. Photo: Haibo Yu

THE VENUE

Finding out where the performance will take place, and what the acting space is going to look like, has top priority for the designer. The size of the stage (if there is one) and the actor–audience relationship are the most influential factors for the final arrangement of this space.

A properly designed acting environment, which includes both stage and auditorium, can make an immediate impression on the audience. As soon as they walk into the space, before the performance even starts, the environment the designer has created will affect them.

Contemporary theatre seldom marks the beginning of the performance by raising the stage curtain. Instead, the audience can see the set on stage, often lit by impressive stage lighting, when they walk into the theatre auditorium. There is no doubt that the director and designer can set a keynote for the performance with this pre-set, and any special treatment of the auditorium, and give a powerful visual signal to the audience before the show begins. Chapter 9 also discusses the importance of venue and space but from another point of view. In theatre-making all points of view must be taken into consideration before a final decision can be reached.

Creating an inspiring environment for the performance is often given serious considera-tion as a crucial part of the design for devised theatre. Obviously, working on low budget, it is impossible to include the whole auditorium, but some minor alterations might be practical and efficient. For example, small-scale extension of the set elements, such as:

- floor texture
- curtains
- hanging objects
- texture or colour on the wall

- lighting effects
- the front-of-house team dressed as characters.

LIMITED SPACES

Providing a workable acting space is one of the primary tasks for any design for the performing arts. However, the physical spaces provided for the company are often disappointing in terms of size, height or shape. In a touring project, the designer has to deal with more potential problems. He has to adapt the spaces in different venues with minimal change to the original design.

TRANSFORMING THE SPACE

The transformation from a fixed and non-workable space to an inspiring and practical space is the most challenging part of the design process. The first challenge a designer has to face is how to provide numerous physical locations. The story may require different locations, possibly with constant transactions between the scenes as well. This is particularly difficult in a devised project, when a low budget and a short construction time bar the designer from using complicated scene-changing techniques, such as trucks or revolving stages, for any rapid scene changes. For the same reason, he has to use the simplest scenic vocabulary to make the set impressive and meaningful. In relation to transforming space, see also Chapter 8, as you will need to consider certain health and safety issues!

Designers tend to answer these extremely demanding circumstances by creating a neutral set. This is an efficient and practical way to serve the multi-location purpose at the lowest cost. Any existing set units in the theatre's storeroom can be altered in colour, texture and shape. If necessary, extra fixed or movable details can be added to make it possible to change the definition of a unit. These neutral units may be re-used as levels, furniture or specific scenic objects, which can be a significant advantage. A set with few specifications can allow performers to transform the space and create the scenes on-stage without relying on set-changes. The audience will experience extra excitement from seeing the lifeless set units transformed into particular objects by actors in an empty space.

SCENIC PARAMETERS AND THEIR CHARACTERISTICS

The designer should provide some set/props parameters for actors at the start of their improvisational experiment and these will vary in form and style according to different acting demands. If no fundamental changes occur during the rehearsal period, these parameters will eventually shape the final design. A list of the most frequently used objects in the devising studio would include: flats, rostra, blocks, fabric, ropes, wooden sticks, weapons, tools. Sometimes more specific objects such as fences, wooden planks, tea chests, tarpaulins or even buckets of water may be called for. When the designer decides what objects to choose as parameters, a series of questions ought to be asked and compared with his predicted vision for the realization of the final design.

The objects selected as parameters are important visual elements for the design. Colour, texture and materials are the three major areas where the designer will wander in search of their external appearance. The visual interpretation of the devised work will be partially created through them. Therefore, apart from practical considerations, they should have a character of their own which is relevant to the work.

The first option is to use scenic elements that have their own specific features and are already connected strongly with the theme. For instance, cardboard boxes and blankets could be used as realistic parameters for devising a piece about homeless people on the street. The second, and more significant possibility, is characterizing highly neutral parameters through the performance, as when actors use ladders to create a mountain scene or a rope to represent a boat.

FLEXIBILITY OF OBJECTS

Another demand for the parameters is that they must be open to variation, i.e. these parameters can be reconstructed into different forms. This is the primary factor for the set's flexibility.

The actors will use the set/props parameters in rehearsal to form and reform the shape of the space. The constant alteration of position, and combinations of the different elements of the set, will create the various scenic contexts for the work. The basic elements may be realistic or abstract in style and in shape, but they must all have the dramatic potential to be changed within seconds to a new shape.

Playing with the basic shapes is great fun, just like playing with a jigsaw puzzle or Lego pieces. For example, if a designer decides to use a triangle (it could be a pure abstract shape or a real A-shape ladder) for the shape of the elementary units, it is not difficult to imagine the numerous possible combinations that could be worked out to create various physical environments, such as mountains, rooftops, a bridge, a ship, a graveyard or a cave.

MOBILITY

The ease with which actors can assemble and reassemble the set during the performance is of

Production of Whale. *Harrogate Theatre, 1998. Director: Chris Baldwin. On the icy-textured white floor, the action created the various scenes with different combinations of four triangles.*

The graveyard.

A helicopter landing on the barge.
Photo: Haibo Yu

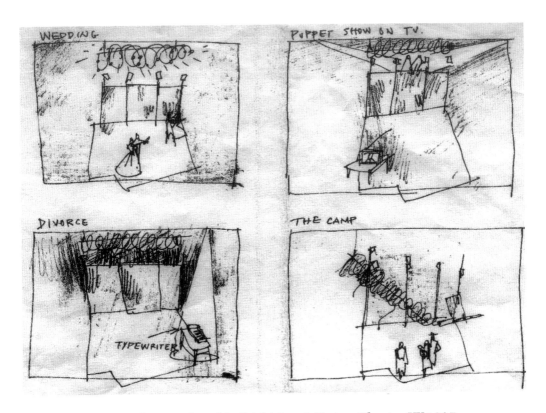

Selected images from the story-board for Bright Angel. Proteus Theatre, UK 1997. *Directors: Chris Baldwin and Bernd Keßler. The predicted scenes are based on a rough scenario.* Photo: Haibo Yu

crucial importance. If certain elements are too big or heavy, the designer must work out a way to make them more mobile – perhaps by fixing casters underneath the structure or subdividing it into smaller units.

OTHER CONSIDERATIONS

The constant concern of designers is human action in a specific space. Devised theatre calls for an intimate communication and interaction between the designer and the actors. Sometimes a designer may consider the actors' positions on the stage as part of the design and use them as human scenery.

Prompt Points

See the exercises at the end of Chapter 1 – they might help you think about how actors within a given space can generate specific responses from an audience.

HUMAN SCENERY

How the actors are positioned, and how they move in the space, can be an important part of the design. This can be viewed from three aspects.

43

Lighting is the most magical tool among the stage techniques. With its flexibility and fluidity, it can change instantly the stage environment and atmosphere.
Photo: Haibo Yu

Position: In an empty space, the desired definition of the area can be presented by the specific positions of the actors; for instance standing in a semi-circle to indicate a round-shape hall.

Grouping: The stage composition and movement on stage are determined by the physical shape of the actors and their positions in relation to each other, to an object and to the audience.

Levels: The position of the actor's body, perhaps standing, bending forward, sitting, kneeling, lying, etc., can be used to create levels to supplement a flat acting space.

LIGHTING

Lighting, an organic part of the design, is the most powerful and flexible tool for changing the stage environment and atmosphere. With its fluidity and flexibility, theatre lighting plays one of the most active roles in devised theatre. Its basic functions include:

* **visibility:** to provide adequate illumination for the acting and make it visible for the audience;
* **selectivity:** to reveal, conceal and balance the different visual aspects on stage;
* **sculpting:** to sculpt the actor's face and body and ensure that they look three-dimensional in the space;

- **fluidity:** to change stage scenes and create atmosphere with the desired pace and rhythm.

Lighting design is a complicated practice, but no matter how much equipment is involved, the basic factors a designer must consider are as follows:

- type of lantern
- angle/distance
- quantity
- intensity
- contrast
- colour
- quality (hard, soft)
- lighting movement (lighting change).

EXERCISES

1. Choose a maximum of two objects to suggest a theatrical location, e.g. a rose window to present a church, a pile of tyres and a jack to suggest a garage.

   Adding an extra object in the designed scene can indicate human's action, even though no one is present, e.g. a bunch of flowers with a card laid at the front door, a police line set up outside a shop.

2. Find the most representative personal props (not costume) for a doctor, a lawyer, a priest, a postman and for other characters.

3. Use nothing but chairs to create as many different locations as you can, e.g. a sitting-room, a waiting lounge, a bus, a boat or even a hill.

4. Create stage pictures using different levels with actors lying, kneeling, sitting, standing and positioned on steps.

5. Position actors in relation to an object, such as a box, a telephone or a door, and find out the interrelated meaning and attitude from their physical relationship to the object.

6. Work with actors in various groupings: one facing two, one and three, actors in a triangle, a circle, diagonal lines, face to face or back to back. Observe and comment on their psychological response to each other as a result of your physical compositions.

3 THE ACTOR-PERFORMER
Sabina Netherclift

Acting for devised theatre requires more from the actor taking part than the interpretation of a well-known role. Actors will need to be comfortable with improvisation, think quickly on their feet and be ready to try out ideas no matter how outlandish. They may need to work in a variety of different ways and styles, some of which may be familiar and some may not. But for a committed actor, working in devised theatre will be one of the most creative experiences they will have as a performer.

The opening moment from Half-Baked Venus' production of Desire Caught by the Tail.
Photo: Jason Hawkes

However, be warned – devised theatre is not for those who want to play lead parts with fantastic amounts of lines. It is, more than any other type of theatre, about being part of a team; we will return to this later on in the chapter.

From the moment an actor auditions, the director will be assessing the way that they work with others, how they play with ideas and how quickly they can turn an idea into a piece of theatre. It is very unlikely that an actor will be expected to prepare a speech and audition formally. Instead they will be invited to a workshop, which may last from two hours to three days, in which they will start to explore some of the themes of the project. Enjoy yourself from the moment you walk through the door. Be as open as you can and rather than worrying about whether you are going to get the job, put yourself 100 per cent into any situation you may be given.

RESEARCH

Different actors use different methods in order to research and perform roles. A written play provides an actor with a framework for her research, with the setting, the language, and the period of the piece all informing her interpretation of a part. Some actors feel that the author gives them all they need to know about the character and prefer to work intensely during rehearsal in order to understand the world of the play or the life of their character. Actors have undertaken to live on the streets, work in publishing firms, set up small communities and interview royalty in order to feel closer to the characters they will eventually inhabit on stage.

This type of research is not exclusive to text-based theatre and can be useful to devising projects in which actors are generating a script that can then be developed or edited by a writer. Dialogue must ring true and whatever kind of theatre you work in as an actor, you will always need to draw on your own experience and observation for inspiration. Every time you read a book, walk down the street or go to the supermarket, you are adding to this experience – every moment of your life will consciously or subconsciously feed into your work. Take notice of the people that you come into contact with every day, formalize this by keeping a notebook of your observations, reflections, thoughts and feelings. There are many inspirations for characterization – passers-by, friends, animals, materials, the elements – but keeping a detailed record of your observations will help you at times when you are feeling 'empty'. You need to keep your creative cupboard well stocked, looking at all things as potential ingredients.

In improvisation I am always looking for an actor who has a true openness. This openness is not merely of the 'Yes! I can do anything!' type. Boundless energy is alas not sufficient. By openness I mean complete trust – trust in the idea of the improvisation, trust in the other improvisers, and trust in the actor's own presence. Trust in the improvisation is of course hugely dependant on the director. Trust in the other performers is dependant on those performers. But trust in the actor's own presence is down to him or her alone. To trust that all you have to do is to be true to the situation you find yourself in, however absurd or unreal, that is the great challenge in the uncertain world of improvisation. If it is not there, improvisation is meaningless. If it is there, it can be miraculous.

David Farr, writer and director.

Having books and other research material in workshops is an invaluable resource for actors.
Photo: Neil Kendall

For specific research on a particular project (a story, newspaper article, poem or book), familiarize yourself with the source material and other relevant pieces that the author has written. It is always useful to be aware of the social and historical context of any piece, even if during the rehearsal process you find that time or place are transposed. Read, but also explore galleries and museums for any light they may shed on society, fashions, political situations and so forth. Make your research fun and something you look forward to – it does not all have to be conducted in a library.

FINAL TIP PRIOR TO REHEARSALS

The up and coming rehearsal process will be a wonderful and creative time, but improvising for eight hours a day can be exhausting. Although it may sound too early, it is worth getting your body into a physical routine before you even start the first day of rehearsals. Spend twenty minutes in the morning doing gentle exercises, anything from stretching, yoga or running to dancing round your room will do the trick. If you can, make sure that you are eating foods that give you energy rather than ones that make you feel sluggish and get used to drinking plenty of water. The fitter you are before you start, the less tiring the rehearsal process (and performances) will be.

REHEARSALS

There is always an element of excitement on starting the first day of a job. The actors in the room with you, possibly all strangers at this stage, will seem very different by the first night. They are all likely to be feeling as you are, although to you they may seem a great deal more confident. Do not forget you are all in the same boat!

More often than not this will be the first time the whole company has met, including the technical and backstage crew. It will be a

---

Prompt Points

See Chapters 1 and 4 in order to discover more about how to work closely with the director and writer. As an actor and performer, you need to bear in mind that while everyone is working hard to get you on stage this does not mean that you can afford to see yourself as more important than anyone else. Read Chapter 6 for more performance related ideas.

---

chance for you to put names to faces, understand what role everyone present has in the project and give the director a chance to outline how the rehearsal schedule will work. This may be particularly important if the director's creative team involves a composer and movement director. You may not see some of the team again until the week before the show opens – the lighting and sound designers may only come back for odd days to get a feel of what is going to happen – so it is good to play a simple game with the entire company to help cement names in everyone's minds.

BEING READY TO PLAY

The first few days may be a process of trying out lots of ideas, not all of which will be developed. Be as open as possible to anything that may be asked of you. It is not helpful to spend a lot of time theorizing about whether certain ideas will work or not. If you do not try them out, you will never know, so try not to get lost in endless debate.

During the first two weeks of rehearsal you will be building trust with your fellow actors and director. Most days will start with a warm-up, physical and vocal, and a game. Games may seem a frivolous way to get going but they are useful for waking people up, establishing the spirit of play essential to improvisation and for getting actors to work quickly as a team. Although two hours of tag is not going to be the best use of your time (you must set a limit on how long you are going to spend warming-up in the morning), games can rescue a day that has run temporarily out of steam. Do not rely on the director to come up with endless suggestions but have a couple of games up your sleeve. The games described later have proved enjoyable ways of getting actors to work well together, whilst making sure they are concentrating and focused on what they are doing.

Actors at the early stages of an improvisation. *Photo: Neil Kendall*

Keep adding to your file of games. Any time you learn a new one write it down. It is surprising how quickly you can forget an old game when something more attractive comes along, so keep a note of everything. It is also important to remember to be considerate of others during games and the improvisations that will take place afterwards.

And this is a gentle warning: if you are working particularly quickly on a project, you will need to build up trust as soon as possible within the company. You must be aware however that there may be certain risks you are willing to take whilst improvising that other cast members would not feel comfortable with. If, for any reason, one member of the cast feels unsafe with another, it will show immediately in the work. If you wish to try something that you know will include physical force, or taking a risk, check with the group

that it is okay to try it out. It is not worth sacrificing a good working relationship for an ill thought-out experiment.

WORKING WITH THE DIRECTING TEAM

The director will structure each day's rehearsal, aided by his creative team. Although different directors will work in different ways, and the amount of rehearsal time available will influence the way that he works, it is not unusual to spend time sketching out the show in fairly broad strokes during the initial period in order to return to more detailed work later.

The director may only be able to give you the bare bones of character or plot to start working from. Use what you know: How old are the characters? What are they? Where are

Game 1: Knock-Kneed Chase

Place as many chairs as there are members of the company around the room. One of the acting company is nominated as 'It', whilst everyone else (A, B, C, D and E in the diagram) takes a seat in the room. There will be one free chair. 'It' stands at the opposite end of the room from the free chair and his or her object is to get to that chair and sit in it. 'It' can only walk (no running) and must walk with his or her knees together. Everyone else has to work together to prevent 'It' from sitting in the free chair, which they do by one of them leaving their seat (in our diagram person C) and occupying the 'It' chair themselves. Once a member of the company has left their seat, they cannot return to it, no matter what, and two people cannot sit on the same chair. However, as

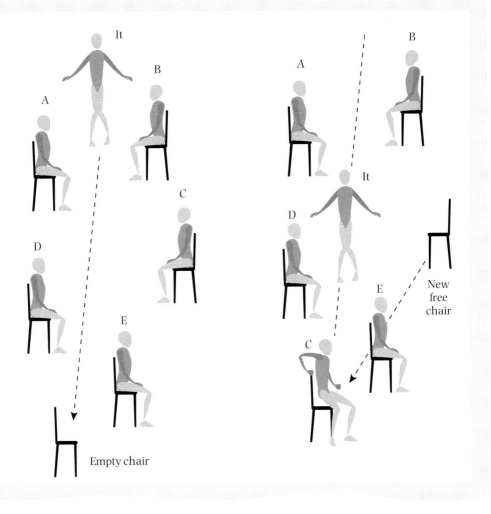

Game 1: Knock-Kneed Chase *continued*

soon as someone has sat in 'It's original target chair, they have left another chair free, which 'It' will now head for. If the company do not work as a team, 'It' will soon find itself a chair that has been too hastily left and the last person to be standing (A), becomes the new 'It'. The game begins again.

Knock-Kneed Chase is all about teamwork. There are certain strategies that will evolve as you play, which will make 'It's job very difficult, and by the time you really know what you are doing, not only will you work as a truly well-oiled machine, but the person playing 'It' should find it impossible to ever sit down.

Game 2: Keep it Up

The second game is very simple – all you will need is a soft but well-sized ball. Start by getting your colleagues into a circle and make sure that they are all awake and concentrating and there are no distractions. When you

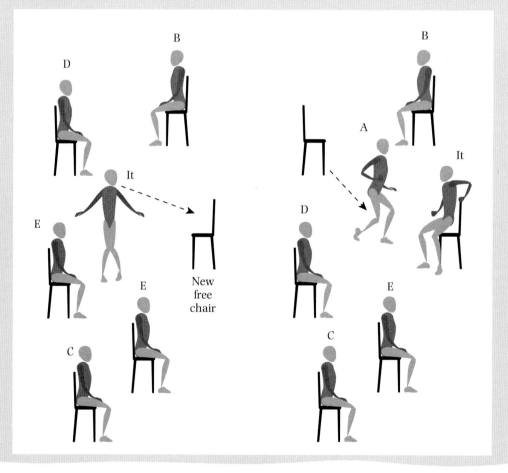

are sure you have total attention, throw the ball in the air and begin to count. It is up to each member of the company to ensure that the ball stays in the air by using their hands or heads to tap it gently upwards. The counting stops if the ball is caught, dropped or bounced off any walls. Each time the ball is successfully kept in the air (and this may involve a great deal of running and diving from the devoted squad) the count goes up. If you can achieve more than fifty any given morning, that is extremely good going!

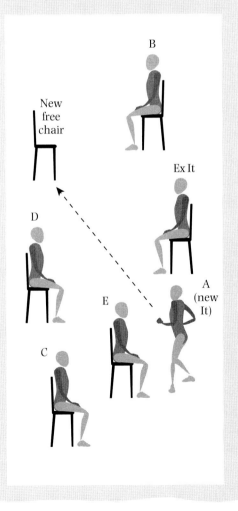

they? What are they doing? Are they with someone else? What is the relationship between them? Why are they there?

If you feel there is not enough information to start building from, ask for more – or make it up! If you are improvising with others, listen. Be open to anything they can give you and give back. Improvising can be difficult; it is not always easy to listen, and it sometimes feels less frustrating to call a halt to proceedings than to stay stuck in the soup of a tricky scene. Keep with it. The director is there to pull things together and keep an eye on the overall shape. Be patient and put your trust in the director's hands. He or she will be feeding you when you feel that the pot is empty.

Always be aware of the space you are working in during scenes. Are you inside or outside? How are you letting the audience know? Are you in a confined space, a busy bar or on a deserted beach? Are you on top of a mountain, or in the underworld? Devised theatre tends to be more visual than most – look for places where you can use all levels available to you, how can you express different perspectives and scales?

If you are lucky enough to be working with a team of stage managers, you may find one of them will sit in during rehearsals taking detailed notes on each day's activities, particularly writing down the moves, so if for any reason you or the director forget what has been decided upon, you have an instant record. However, this is a luxury in devised theatre and the reality will probably be one harassed stage manager having to accomplish several tasks at the same time.

Although many actors have physical memories, which allow them to remember blocking in relation to actions, the position of other actors and so forth, some find it necessary to keep a personal record of where they moved, when and with whom. Always remember to pack a pencil when you go to

Actors improvising and creating different spaces. Photo: Neil Kendall

Experimenting with levels. Photo: Neil Kendall

rehearsals, just in case you need to start scribbling half way through.

You may find it useful to go over scenes by 'marking' them out. This simply means that you go through the movements and text of a scene without doing them in full or giving the words any emphasis – but simply as a way of fixing actions and timings. It is incredibly helpful to do this as rehearsals progress, possibly taking ten minutes at the start of each day to make sure work from the day before has stuck in place.

WORKING WITH DESIGNERS

You will often find that one designer will be responsible for both the set and costume design in devised theatre. This may be due to financial reasons but more usually is a deliberate artistic decision to ensure overall coherence in the finished design and feel of the piece. Read Chapter 2 and Chapter 7 for more insights into how actors can find invaluable help with character development from designers in the devising process.

Having the costume designer present during the early stages of rehearsals is extremely helpful for an actor, particularly if the show is to be improvised from scratch or involves one actor playing several characters.

Some designers may turn up with completed sketches and the costumes they produce may work very well within the production, but collaboration is the best method to achieve costumes that are functional and helpful to the actors as well as fitting into the overall design

It is always a bonus when devising, if the designer brings costume and props for the actors to play with. Get stuck in and experiment with skirts and trousers, padding and stuffing, sheets and materials, dolls and puppets, anything that the designer has brought along to help you develop characters and scenes. If the designer has brought pen,

Actors working as a chorus in the background act as a counterpoint to the central character.

paper and Sellotape, improvise your own props.

Being involved in the rehearsal process provides me, as a designer, with a rich source of inspiration. Watching the actors working on the physical and mental processes of revealing a character, allows me to create an environment, which responds directly to the performance as it evolves, rather than imposing ideas from the outside.

Sarah Blenkinsop, Designer

55

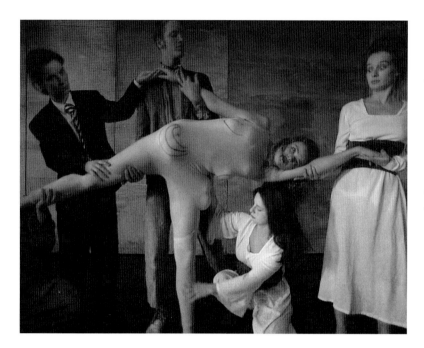

Working with the costume designer led the tart in this production of Picasso's Desire Caught by the Tail *to wear a practical costume, which also suggested the style of Picasso's painting. Director: Jasper Britton.*
Photo: Jason Hawkes

An actor is playing a character that moves partly on the floor and partly standing upright. She experiments with a skirt that feels right and influences her with the development of one aspect of the character's movement. The skirt is very full and suggests to the actor that the character (who is unpleasant and enjoys doing unpleasant things) does so in a graceful and almost elegant way. However, the skirt greatly impedes the actress in her ability to get up and down to the floor quickly. The designer is able to create a costume that addresses all the above needs.

If you are for any reason unsure about a particular costume idea, in terms of the way you have been developing a particular character, it is important to express your concerns as soon as possible. You have to feel comfortable wearing whatever has been designed for you, and it is preferable to indicate early on if you feel that inappropriate decisions are being made, rather than to wait until you have a fully fitted costume, which may be expensive to remake.

USING PROPS

Having props available to play with is a wonderful bonus when devising theatre. There may be advantages in using puppets to play certain characters or in using props to represent other objects, particularly if the director is trying to suggest a sense of scale to the audience. The terror of a small boat being tossed about in an angry and unforgiving sea may be communicated more effectively with a tiny paperclip being manipulated by an actor on the billows and swells of a large sheet, than by trying to recreate the scene using actors behaving naturalistically. Such solutions are great fun and will extend your capabilities as a performer but will require dedicated rehearsal time to pull off effectively. It is important to be

The lead character's basic and simple costume provides a stark contrast to the other characters' more extraordinary outfits. Photo: Neil Kendall

very aware of where the focus lies in such work and this can present challenges to actors unused to working in this way.

It is incredibly useful to play around with ideas of scale within devised theatre. Exercising your imaginative use of props is something you can do both in and out of the rehearsal room. See Chapter 7, Exercise 3 for more ideas on props and actors.

Find objects at home that you can manipulate in different ways, e.g. umbrellas as birds, boats or shields. How many different imaginative uses for an everyday object can you find? Play with the objects that are lying around the rehearsal room at odd times when you are not working. You never know when something might strike you.

WORKING WITH A COMPOSER

Working with a composer, much as with a designer, will depend on how music is to feature in the piece. Generally, if music is just atmospheric, you may meet the composer briefly but rarely work with him (or her). However, if music is integral to a show, the composer will probably attend auditions to ensure that everyone in the cast has the necessary level of musicality. This may mean actual ability to play an instrument or sing, or being able to respond sensitively to rhythms or the character of a piece of music. In the latter case, you will need to be as open to playing with music as you are to playing with your fellow actors, and the composer's ideas may be as

Actors use food and cutlery to tell part of the story in this improvisation.

I've found that the best devisers needn't play an instrument themselves. Some of my favourite actors to work with have barely a grade 1 recorder exam between them. In addition to the essential skills you might expect (patience, good musical memory, confidence, risk-taking), the ability I find most useful is the ability to 'play' with the music – as if it were another character on stage; to experiment with the effect that the music is having on the scene, or their character, and to invent games to play with it spontaneously. Sometimes this requires a leap of faith in the actor who loses control of the tempo of the drama to the score - but it is a leap worth taking.

Paul Clark, composer and musical director, Clod Ensemble

theatrical as your improvisations are musical. See Chapter 5 for more ideas on how musicians, performers and composers can work together and often even be indistinguishable!

Again, the golden rule – be prepared to try things out. It may be that you will be improvising with music already written or that the composer will be with you in rehearsal and will come up with melodies and rhythms that may help the pace of a scene or set a particular tone. For example, the regimented tedium of an office scene may be helped by actors drumming a repetitive rhythm on their desks or the sleazy atmosphere of a late night jazz club be conjured up by five lazy notes on a saxophone.

THE MOVEMENT DIRECTOR

Movement directors are usually brought on board when a show has a very strong stylistic

Actors working to create a highly choreographed chorus of boredom.
Photo: Jason Hawkes

element: this can be anything from helping a cast to capture the essence of animals (e.g. Wind in the Willows), to choreographing battle scenes or working with the chorus within Greek drama. If they are working with you regularly, they may well lead you for a warm up at the beginning of the day. Enjoy this time! Movement directors have usually developed compact and efficient sets of exercises that will serve you well when they have gone and the run has started. Pick up everything you can and, of course, apply the golden rule – be open to their direction. See Chapter 6 for further detailed suggestions on how movement can become a key visual and story-making element in a devised show.

FINAL STAGES OF REHEARSAL AND PERFORMANCE

If you have been working to schedule, you should feel relatively prepared as the technical

and dress rehearsals and first night approach. The technical rehearsal is a necessary evil for actors. Although much of the plotting for lights and sound should be completed by the time the actors are called, there are often unavoidable delays and actors may have to wait for a long time before they are required. Be patient. The technical crew will have been working very long hours during this time and will be unappreciative of any gripes you may have. Although there may be periods during which you will not be needed to mark positions or be present on stage, always make sure that the stage manager or DSM knows where you are. There is nothing more frustrating for the director than trying to find an actor who has just popped to the shops for some tea.

The dress rehearsal will be a chance to put everything together before the first night. It may not be perfect and will highlight any technical changes that still need to be made. You may find costume changes that take too

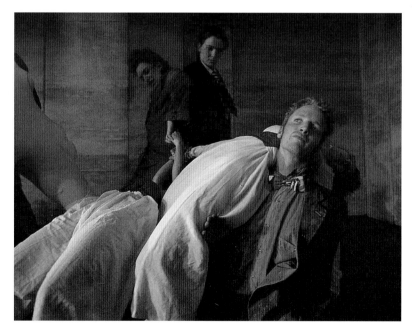

This scene of **Desire Caught by the Tail** *involved one actor carrying the weight of two others. Scenes such as these must be rehearsed with great care and need only be marked through in technical rehearsal.*
Photo: Jason Hawkes

long or particular props prove to be more awkward on stage than expected. Many of these difficulties get ironed out during the run. The more you practise with costume and props, the easier everything becomes.

It is sometimes the case that not everything has been finished by the technical and dress rehearsals. This is an inevitable by-product of creating a show from scratch. Do not panic. Some devised shows may need to change once they are in front of an audience. There may be scenes that simply do not work in the theatre and the director may rework certain areas and totally cut others. It is important as an actor to be prepared for this possibility. Although you may become attached to a piece of work in which you have invested a great deal of yourself, you must trust the director to make informed decisions and accept any changes made to make the show better. After that, it is down to you! Enjoy yourself!

EXERCISES

Exercise 1: Character through Physicality – Leading with Different Parts of the Body

Start off standing in a room in your house. Imagine that an invisible cord attached to your nose is pulling you around the space. Allow yourself to be led by your nose around the room and into other areas of your house. Notice as you are being pulled by your nose what other areas of your body are compensating. Does walking in the position you are in feel more comfortable if you are walking quickly or slowly? If you can, take a look at yourself in the mirror. Find a single adjective that might describe that character and write it down in your notebook. Repeat the exercise using different areas of your face, Lead with your forehead. What differences do you notice between leading with the nose and the forehead? Where do you have to

compensate in the rest of your body, if you are leading yourself around by your forehead? Lead with your chin. Experiment with leading with your chest and then your belly. How does leading with the chest and belly affect the way you move? Notice, when you are next out for a walk, if you can see anyone who is leading with a particular part of their body. How does it affect the way that they walk? What kind of rhythm do they move in, fast or slow? Jot anything interesting down in your notebook.

Exercise 2: Finding Character through Physicality

Go to the zoo or a park. Take your notebook and choose four different animals to study. Look at the way each one moves, noticing the rhythm of their movements. Is there any pattern to their movements? (For example, Meerkats' movements range from standing very upright on two legs, with their two front paws resting in front of their bodies, looking about them intently, to swift and sharp movements that allow them to disappear in an instant). Notice which part of their bodies lead them – does a wolf lead with his shoulders or his knees? Does his head hang high or low? Does he move slowly or fast, does a giraffe have the same rhythm as a wolf? What part of the body does he lead from? Notice the difference in rhythm of different animals and put it all in your notebooks.

Take your researches back home and experiment with building a human character on an animal base. Pick a creature that you have studied closely and finding a space, start walking as that animal – go down on to all fours if you can and try to be as accurate with its movements as physically possible. When you feel that you have captured its movement and rhythms, start to reduce the level of animal you are playing and increase your human movements. Carry on with this process until you are upright and walking about with just the merest trace of the animal left. It may be the hanging shoulders and head of a wolf, or the sharp and quick head movements of the squirrel. Imagine situations for these characters, e.g. at an office or in a dentist's waiting-room, and try playing with each one in the same situation. Find a voice for your character. Put two of your characters (e.g. a wolf and a sheep) into the same situation (the dentist and patient perhaps) and see how quickly you can change from one to the other. There will be essential keys that you will discover as you work that will immediately distinguish one character from another.

You will have many resources to draw on whilst improvising and the ideas above are just suggestions that might help you. Inspiration for characters can come from people you know or more obscure sources but all of it is relevant. Keep your eyes open and keep adding to your stores.

Exercise 3: Experimenting with Scale

Find a story that appeals to you, with a cast of at least three characters and a good setting – Aesop's fables are a good place to look. Empty your kitchen drawers and cupboards and experiment with telling the story using only cutlery, cooking spoons, some pans and a sieve. Tell the story again using only vegetables and fruit, and then tell it again using a mixture of food and implements. Try to be as imaginative as possible in the way you use whatever objects you have assembled. You will make lots of discoveries by experimenting with storytelling in this way and many of them might surprise you. By experimenting at home you are adding to the resources you can draw on in the rehearsal room and if you have been unused to approaching objects in this way, a little home experimentation will allow you to build your confidence in just trying things out.

Actors playing with masks, coats and scarves. Photo: Neil Kendall

4 PLAYWRITING

Bernd Keßler

Ever since Aristotle, the word 'plot' has existed in the world of theatre. The plot is the bringing together, the arrangement, of actions and is thus at the centre of all the performing arts. But constructing a line of playable actions is not enough to develop an interesting plot. When an audience sits down in a theatre space, it comes with expectations. It will not wish to be informed (there are better mediums for this) so much as entertained and, most importantly, to be surprised. A good theatre plot always contains a surprise for the audience, whether it is the death of Cordelia in Shakespeare's *King Lear*, Katrin being shot in Brecht's *Mother Courage* or an interesting turn of events in a soap opera. The main responsibility of a playwright in a devising context, therefore, is to work with the director and actors to ensure that an interesting, surprising plot is generated from the source material.

It is no coincidence that many famous dramatists, including Shakespeare, Goethe, Molière and Brecht, worked with actors during the early periods of text development and rehearsal in the same way as many devising companies do today. And it is fascinating to note that Shakespeare took little or no interest in seeing his plays into print. For him, working with actors in order to test the resilience and effectiveness of his texts in front of an audience in the theatre was his first priority.

Along with a director and actors, the playwright can generate a line of actions which will, in time, constitute the spine of the play. Once the script has been written, actors can also help the writer see that parts of the story are missing or exist without sufficient motivation, and that some actions or moments simply will not work when seen by the audience.

It might seem that we can write plays in the same way as we rehearse – in other words, completely collectively; ideas, associations and experiences from different directions can flow into the text from the whole company and make it richer. But it is probably the case that once all these influences and ideas have been heard and explored, one person must hold the pen and fix the words on the paper.

See Chapter 1 for more ideas about developing 'lines of action' in rehearsal, and Chapter 2 for how fundamental decisions regarding a set can alter the way a story can be told.

FIRST STAGES OF RESEARCH AND DEVELOPMENT:

Locating the first idea for the story, one that will be the base for the early phase of development and rehearsal, is a crucial task for any devising team and one in which the writer must take a leading role from the very outset.

The story being developed may have a surprising starting point. For example, the discovery that a secret exists between a husband and wife can lead to a huge revelation. Or it may be a concern for a social

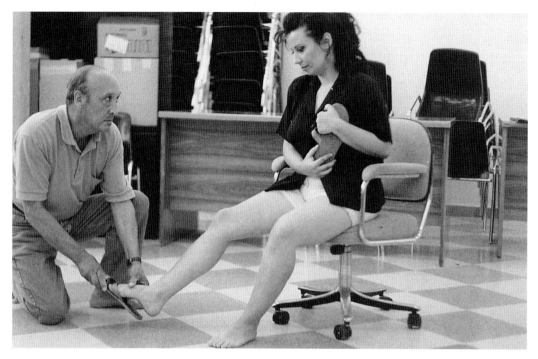

Pre-rehearsal workshops with actors can help in finding the key moments in a story. Bright Angel *devising workshop with actors, Cuidad Real, Spain, 1996.*
Photo: Fernando Bercebal

Snake Pits !

Whatever the starting point, the playwright must protect against allowing one of the characters to become the mouthpiece for his/her or the company or director's opinions, or allow a character to promote his/her or their beliefs and values. This is a snake pit into which we can all fall!

One character can never present the position of the author (e.g. warning, encouraging, educating, presenting a solution, suggesting rebellion or resignation or an invitation to sing together!). Instead the whole work must contain the position of the playwright and company or the statement that they wish to make.

or political theme or situation that the playwright and company are particularly interested in.

STAGE ONE: INVENTING THE CHARACTERS

At first glance it might seem odd to think about actions between characters before turning to the characters themselves. And of course, while it is impossible to develop the action between characters unless we know something about the characters first, it is surprising how little we need to know before work can begin. This is because the audience only begins to understand dramatic character by how that character responds within playable moments. The situation is a bit 'chicken and egg', and it is sometimes difficult to see where to begin. So let us take one concrete situation and examine how a simple playable action can lead the playwright and devising team to learn more about the characters. (Chapter 3 offers a valuable yet contrasting point of view in regards to inventing characters.)

Inventing a Simple Situation or 'Playable Action'

For example: the silence of a man (Tomas) at the moment of the unexpected death of his wife (Rachel).

This is the moment the playwright, director and acting team want to explore in the rehearsal room. One actress is asked to be the dead woman. But the actress playing Rachel simply replies 'how can I play "dead"?'. It is possible, but before being able to do so, four concrete questions must be asked and answers located:

Finding Playable Actions

Example of a weak playable action: A man, sitting on a park bench, opens his lunch box. He unwraps a sandwich and begins to eat it. A second man sits down and begins to read a newspaper. The first man says, 'It is so peaceful here'. The second man says, 'I agree!' and then begins to read from the newspaper. The man eating the sandwich closes his lunch box and leaves. The man reading the newspaper gets up a moment later and exits in the opposite direction.

Example of a stronger playable action: A man, sitting on a park bench, opens his lunch box. He unwraps a sandwich and begins to eat it. A second man sits down and begins to read a newspaper. The first man says, 'It is so peaceful here'. The second man says, 'I agree!' and then begins to read aloud from the newspaper.

While these two examples are very simple, the second reveals a contradiction between the two men and thus presents something that could develop into a surprising and entertaining crisis.

- Where was Rachel before she died? (Past)
- Where was she when she died? (Present)
- Where was she going when she died? (Future)
- Where do we join the story? (The playable moment).

As you will see, the four questions each relate to a time context: past, present, future and what does the audience see? None of us live entirely in the present. We are often as concerned with what we will be doing in one hour's time, as much as what we are doing in this moment. And for many, what has happened in the past will affect what is happening in the present and what will happen in the future. So the director, actress and playwright must find answers to these questions. Let us imagine the answers.

- Where was Rachel before she died? (Past)
  - A year ago: at university taking her final year.
  - A month ago: getting married to Tomas, the boy she fell in love with at university.
  - An hour ago: discovering that her sister, Anna, was pregnant.

As you will see there are different time spans to consider – each one adding important information to the situation.

- Where was she when she died? (Present)
  - The morning: She left home at 8.30am and drove to her sister's house for breakfast. Over breakfast her sister, Anna, tells her the good news – she is pregnant. They were both ecstatic!
  - After breakfast: She left her sister's house at midday and drove to work. She parked her car in the garage below her office. As she walked out of the garage... (you, the reader, can devise the 'how' for yourself)...she is killed.

- Where was Rachel going when she died? Again this question has a series of answers – we need to look at the short, medium and long term:
  - Where was she going in the next ten minutes?
  - Where was she going to be over the next few weeks?
  - Where was she hoping to be going over the next few years?

Some of the answers to these questions may be very concrete indeed. 'She was going to write an e-mail at her computer' may be the answer to the first question. But the answer to the final question might be 'She was hoping to use her degree in French to be transferred from the London office to Paris'.

And then we need to ask the same question for the other characters:

- Where was Tomas, her husband, before his wife died? (Past)
- Where was Tomas when she died? (Present)
- Where was he going when she died? (Future)

Clearly the rehearsal process needs to find answers to these questions. But here is where chance and imagination is crucial and the director, writer and actor-performer can transform a small moment in rehearsal. For the sake of this exercise, let us just imagine that at the moment that Rachel dies, the devising team play with the idea that Tomas is with Anna, Rachel's sister. We will come back to this later.

Where Do We Join the Story?
At the beginning of this chapter we said that the plot is the bringing together, the arrangement, of actions. It is thus at the centre of all our work as dramatists. And this is why all four questions relate to action (e.g.

All characters need a past, present and potential future. **Bright Angel.** *Proteus*
Theatre, UK 1997. Directors: Chris Baldwin and Bernd Keßler. Photo: Jeremy Pakes

where was/is she going?) What we see
happening, as an audience, and the sequence
in which we see it happening, will determine
our sympathies or empathies towards the
characters in the play.

It may be that we join the story at the point
at which Rachel meets Tomas, her husband to
be, for the very first time. This way, at the point
at which she dies, the audience will have
already learnt a lot about her and will quite
possibly feel deeply shocked at her death. But if
the audience were to join the story at the
moment she gets out of the car in the garage
below her office, then the audience might feel
shock and surprise, but this would quickly
turn into a series of questions:

- Who is this woman?
- Why was she coming out of the garage?
- Where was she going?
- Why should we care about her?

Other Characters

The same four questions asked of Rachel and
Tomas need to be repeated for all the other
characters in the story. But this is where we
need to be conscious of Stage Two of the
process.

Utilizing the Unexpected

Sometimes something small happens in
rehearsal that can transform the whole
process. Recognizing these moments, and

devising, and transforming them into successful performance outcomes, is a key skill not only for the writer and director, but indeed, for the whole team. But such small happenings come out of concrete situations. In Chapter 7 you will also read about how unexpected discoveries can provide some of the richest results in final performance.

STAGE TWO: LOOKING FOR THE 'PLAYABLE ACTIONS'

Once we have our characters, we can begin to look at what they do, the sequence in which they do them and the degree to which the audience knows about all this. Let us examine the story we are developing between our characters Tomas and Rachel. Where exactly was Tomas when Rachel died and does this hold a clue as to where the story might go next?

The playwright needs to be very nosy indeed – putting his or her nose into the business of all the emerging characters: this is what must concern him first and foremost in the very early devising rehearsals. So it would be a good to ask, 'Why was Tomas with his wife's sister, Anna, ten minutes after Rachel, his wife, left? And why was he still there when Rachel died?'. This is the kind of intriguing question that the playwright, director and performers will explore in a series of improvisations. In other words, the improvisations are aimed at exploring the nature of the 'playable action'. It might turn out to be the kind of question that will provoke a significant development within the show.

Playable Action – Words and Silence

There are many examples of non-verbal theatre, and thus examples of playable actions that do not require words, working highly effectively. From mime to physical theatre, companies have discovered the power of drama as other than just the spoken word. As a result, such work crosses cultural frontiers effortlessly. If the playwright is insistent that everything must be packed into words and that these words must be packed into the mouths of characters, then the writer is working in the wrong genre. To reinforce this point, read a libretto for an opera or a script for dance theatre. There we find the appropriate foundations that drama essentially requires – a presentation of the action or a description of what happens independent of whether a character speaks or not.

STAGE THREE: EXTENDING THE 'PLAYABLE ACTIONS' BY FINDING CONTRADICTIONS

What provokes or releases the potential for a dramatic moment? What is the underlying force that enables us to develop a story for the stage? As we have seen, stage one of the devising process is concerned with character, and stage two with locating a series of 'playable actions'. Every playwright who has attempted to write a drama knows that different characters will need to be invented and that they will meet in the play. And when these characters meet, they will have different histories, different needs, different desires and expectations. In other words, their histories, needs, desires and expectations may occasionally, or better still for theatre, profoundly, clash against one another. The motor for the theatre play is the presentation and settling of the contradictions between people. Only through the discovery of contradictions, and bringing them into the play, is the writer developing a dramatic work. Contradictions move the characters around the stage and thus they exist at all stages and levels of our work – the most significant level being between different characters.

Contradiction Between Characters

Let us explore further our story of Rachel and Tomas. Imagine, for example, that the night before the death of Rachel, she arrives home early from work. Convinced that Tomas is acting strangely, she asks him if he is feeling well. Unbeknown to her, her sister is hiding upstairs in the bedroom. Whatever the situation, the actors, director and playwright must give these characters different opinions and motivations from the beginning of the situation. As it progresses, they will all develop their own opinions about how this crisis is best settled. All these ideas can be discovered collectively in a devising rehearsal process led by the director and playwright, and yet it is probably the playwright who will bring the story together into a unified whole on paper.

Knowing how to recognize and utilize the notion of 'contradiction' is a crucial skill for all directors and writers. See Chapter 1 for more information on this subject from another point of view. Chapter 2 and Chapter 5 also discuss how design and music can contradict action or audience expectation, and thus make the audience work harder.

Contradictions Within Character

The next level is the one in which contradictions within one character are presented, for example, between what a character says and what we see him or her do. Taking our example of Rachel and her sister Anna. Let us imagine we were to see the husband, Tomas, announce at the beginning of the play that he loves his wife more than anything in the world. But, after the scene in which the two sisters have breakfasted together, we see him at Anna's apartment telling her that he will divorce Rachel and marry her. A dramaturgically interesting structure containing surprises is beginning to emerge.

Surprise

How can the devising team, guided by a playwright, surprise an audience and present something unexpected? Stripteases, buckets of blood and excrement, nakedness, brutality or the celebration of perversities can no longer surprise. The audience has probably seen it all. The playwright needs to look deeper for the surprising solution. Everyone knows the power of a punch line in a well-told joke – theatre plots work in the same way. The surprise becomes possible by leading the audience through a carefully crafted and constructed series of scenes up to, and through, a totally unexpected turning point. It is the existence of turning points that will force the audience to reassess everything that has come before. This is where the power of surprise lies.

In the devising rehearsal, it is the role of the playwright, assisted by the director and actors, to look for, and ultimately agree, a series of 'playable moments/actions'. As rehearsal progresses it becomes the primary responsibility of the director to translate these playable actions into a performance. It is simply not the case that making theatre, devised or scripted, is achieved by providing dialogue and by describing the place in which such dialogue takes place. This is where devising and working collaboratively with a director, designer and actors, are a great help to the writer. Actors are able to create a room simply by the way they enter a space. It is a serious error to discuss the suggestions rather than rehearsing them. The writer and the director will produce a stronger piece in the end if they arrive at a script by rehearsing rather than by talking about things.

WORKING ALONE

Once the devising team have devised a series of characters with histories, been led by the playwright to locate 'playable actions' for these characters and extended these actions by looking for internal and external contradictions, the playwright can retire to write down the scene. This may be no more than simply recording what has already been discovered in rehearsal or it may be the point at which still unresolved problems need the special attention of the writer. Whatever the situation, the primary role of theatre text is to indicate what is to happen in each given moment. Language is important as it tells an audience about how characters think, their class, race and gender backgrounds. But the writer must know how few words need to be written too!

Unlikely Playable Actions

Silence can be a playable action – a task not easy for the actor as there is no such thing as an abstract silence in theatre. It can only present playable concrete actions. The writer needs, therefore, to help the devising actor by looking for 'concrete silences', for example:

- The silence of a man at the moment of the unexpected death of his wife.
- The silence of the student at the moment she receives an unexpected question from her teacher.
- The silence of the goalkeeper as he looks at the ball at the back of the net.

Theatre presents concrete actions that happen between people. If we think about the three examples above, of silent yet playable actions, we see that they must be played in three totally different ways. With these ideas in mind, we have collected some fundamental notions or elements, which describe what must be the base of a theatre text.

BRINGING THE TEXT BACK TO REHEARSALS

The writer has worked well into the night and produced the new scene for the next day's rehearsal. Trying out the new scene is like test-driving a new car. The maker of this new vehicle has the opportunity to learn which parts grind, stick or completely fail to function altogether. If things are grinding and sticking, then clearly the writer needs to look at possible reasons. Is the scene too long? Does it include unnecessary dialogue? Look for how, by removing unnecessary dialogue, the scene can function more effectively and allow the action of the scene to emerge more strongly.

During these first hours with a fresh script, the playwright needs to observe where and how the actors and director propose cuts, and look for ways to make the text shorter and easier, both to speak and to understand. He must be ready to accept that some text and passages will not find their way into the final performance – often a painful experience. But in many such cases, these cuts will be healthy for both the play and the performance. The playwright will also have the opportunity to see how the actors begin to use their skills upon the script – displaying, in one look or one action, what half a page of writing cannot achieve. When the writer sees this happen, he must allow the script to change accordingly. He must also ensure that repetition is avoided, unless it is designed for a purpose, and be ruthless with the unnecessary repetition that is an inherent danger in devised work. The writer can collect and re-work valuable experience that is impossible to learn from the page alone.

The glance between two women says more than a thousand words. Bright Angel.
Proteus Theatre, UK 1997. Directors: Chris Baldwin and Bernd Keßler.
Photo: Jeremy Pakes

In the first collective reading of the play, and during early rehearsals, an actor will try to make the text belong to him – he will want to change it to make the script more speakable. During this phase, the writer can also test which sentences and passages feel organic and which artificial.

As you write your script you can often become hugely excited about how the characters are coming alive. But caution is required! At times like this your imagination might invent various spurious activities for the characters – 'she drinks from her cup of coffee', 'cleans the room', 'smokes a cigarette' – actions that are anything other than compelling or urgent. Stage directions of this nature damage a play more than they help because the fantasy of the actors and directors, which is required to bring the play alive on stage, is stifled. But much more dangerous for the play is that the attention paid to these kind of actions results in a curtain being drawn across the important and central actions of the play. The majority of famous playwrights, from Shakespeare to Brecht, renounced such instructions – the fewer the better, as a quick glance at *King Lear* will tell us. Instead you must trust the stage and lighting designers, directors, actors, carpenter and technical teams to do their jobs.

The theatre is a place where reality, or invented experiences of reality, are presented.

Prompt Points

The selection of events and opinions, and their inclusion in the form of dialogue between people, is no guarantee for a good theatre text. The playwright must be on the look-out in rehearsal for situations (or playable moments) that seem interesting. Gradually, from these moments, a plot will need to develop based on the characters and the contradictions they face. This is probably best done in conjunction with the director. See the exercises in Chapter 1.

It is the task of the playwright to discover or invent a series of underlying actions or situations which, in turn, can be played by actors. The scenario of Rachel, her husband Tomas and her sister Anna is an example of how what the audience sees, and the sequence in which it is seen, is as important as anything they listen to. This, over and above the production of words, is the playwright's prime task. Texts for the theatre are suggestions for playing and not first and foremost, for speaking. Before the playwright begins to write anything on paper, he must have already settled upon a series of actions on which everything else will be based – something made all the more easy in a devising context. The task of the playwright is to bury the action within the dialogue. Of course it is easier to say this than to put it into practice but all playwrights, both within the devising context and elsewhere, must guard against there being insufficient action. Dramatic literature uses a very subtle method for enabling the actors to do their work. The prerequisite for the development of playing actions is the existence of different characters that meet on the stage and clash (we will talk about monologues later – a special case in which one actor meets his or her public).

Two different historical moments (a policeman writing a report and the fall of the Berlin Wall) are combined to make one theatrical moment. **Bright Angel.** *Proteus Theatre, UK 1997. Directors: Chris Baldwin and Bernd Keßler.* Photo: Jeremy Pakes

WHO ARE THE REAL PLAYERS IN THEATRE?

Who are the people that will play out the story worked out in rehearsals? At first sight the answer to this question seems a very easy, logical, straightforward one. It seems to be clear that actors have the main task to make the story come alive, accompanied by the director and the production team. But an important player, maybe the most important player, is often forgotten: the main player in theatre is the audience.

Theatre without spectators is nonsense. Of course some might ask why we should think about the audience at all. There are two traditions that would question the responsibility and ability of the playwright to enter into a meaningful dialogue with an audience. One, perhaps best described as the inheritor of the nineteenth-century view of the artist as romantic individualist, sees it as being the audience' responsibility to try to understand what the artist presents. The other, the late twentieth-century post-modernist position, would see the attempt at meaningful dialogue between play and spectators as futile and random at best. But both views are rejected here. The playwright and company do usually have an idea or message which, by writing and producing a drama, can be brought to an audience. We already know that there can be different motivations (to warn entertain, etc.), but the theatre writer is attempting a very special mediation. He has chosen not to write propaganda leaflets to be thrown out of a plane; he has chosen to write a drama for the theatre. And when writing for theatre there are quite different working principles than for when writing a novel or a poem.

First, theatre is an agreement between those who prepare a show and their audience. This agreement says: at a special time the spectators will come to an agreed place, for example a theatre building, and at this place something will be presented by the actors that will be entertaining, may have profound significance, and possibly have a message. During this time the actors present an image of reality without it actually being reality. It will only exist for as long as the actors and production team take to present their work. Then it is gone. It can live longer, but only by being carried away in the memory of the audience. The audience has to observe the presented action and experience the intentions of those who make the production. The spectators come to the theatre with many expectations, which begin to unfold even before the curtain (if there is one) rises.

Should the performance be a monologue, they sit expectantly in their seats as partners to the performer. If 500 or 1,000 people at the same time watch a performance, every spectator has a different experience. Each one of them is the product of different levels of education, cultural expectations, age, and life experience. The ability to observe is different in all and is mediated by very personal components, such as sensibility, receptiveness and the ability to bring their own associations to the experience, and finally their mood at the time of the theatre visit. As theatre-makers we must take all these elements into our calculations. But over and above this, the playwright must remember that the audience will contain thinking people who will experience, and process for themselves, the playable actions on stage.

The intellectual and emotional collaboration of the audience during the performance is a crucial part of the theatre experience. The well-informed dramatist, as he writes the play, considers these points. This does not mean that he must pander to the tastes of the audience – not at all. It is at this level that another stratum of contradictions begins to emerge – contradictions that need to be

LIVERPOOL COLLEGE
LRC

73

mobilized through the text. Playwrights need to locate the contradictions that exist between the actions of the characters on the stage, and the knowledge and life experience of the audience. This is probably the most sophisticated and interesting level at which contradictions operate in the theatrical event.

THE WORST CRIME IN THEATRE

If the devised play, indeed any play, only presents things that the audience already knows well, the audience will soon become bored. And boredom is the worst crime in theatre. It is the task of the playwright, the director and the actors to do everything possible to activate the contradictory voices inside the head of every member of the audience. Only in a theatre performance does the audience work in this way and, with luck, they will take away with them unforgettable and cherished memories of these moments.

What resource has a playwright to hand in order to ensure that the audience becomes co-creators in theatre? I have already said that he can ensure that the characters act in such a way that the audience cannot agree with their actions and thus resist or contradict them. Also, we can attract and maintain the attention of the audience by presenting a contrast between what a character says and what a character does. An old trick of dramatists, with the help of time shifts or omissions between scenes or acts, is to force the audience to fill in the gaps in the plot for themselves. This can be done by, for example, beginning the play after the action has already started or finishing the play before the action ends. The audience must thus fill the gaps and become co-creators of the story.

When all the playable actions have been presented then, and only then, should the actor open his mouth and allow words to come out. The text, or the word, is the last resort of the theatre.

It is very easy to compose a theatre play: you simply construct a line of playable actions, add many contradictions into the mix, glue it together into an understandable plot and then look for a really big surprise to be placed at the crucial turning point. Or maybe.

As two characters manipulate a puppet they fall in love. **Bright Angel. Proteus Theatre, UK 1997. Directors: Chris Baldwin and Bernd Keßler.** *Photo: Jeremy Pakes*

5 MUSIC AND COMPOSITION
Paul Barker

Devising music for theatre is largely a process of digesting questions – the longer that answers are delayed, the more chance there may be of organic creative growth among the company. Somehow, the instinctive need we all have for immediate, utilitarian answers has to be replaced by the energy that individuals discover when fully engaging their imagination and creativity. For that reason, the structure of this chapter is a series of provocative questions. The questions themselves are capable of being answered in an infinite variety of ways, and the answers here can only be partial. Furthermore the same questions, when articulated constantly throughout the process of devised theatre – in pre-production meetings, production meetings, rehearsals and performances – may help each member of the company feel they have something unique to offer, through experience or imagination.

Music is more dependent upon notions of right and wrong than any other art form. In the theatre, the pursuit of right and wrong may restrict the composer's imagination and creativity. Later, much later in the process of devised theatre, the concepts of right and wrong may be replaced by appropriate and inappropriate, but that is only possible after thoroughly considering the possible and pushing at the barriers of the impossible.

People tend to perceive music from one of two extremes: self-assurance or lack of confidence. Both may be limiting in a collaborative theatrical situation where the musical language has yet to be discovered alongside the theatrical language. Experienced classical/jazz/rock/folk musicians may feel unable to work outside their own specialized style, which may be inappropriate to the final theatrical style. Their obvious expertise and fluency may be a barrier to the confidence of a novice with imagination but no technique. So we will assume, for the purpose of this chapter, simply that the reader wishes to be, or is about to be, involved in a devised project and has some responsibility for music, irrespective of their experience and background.

WHAT IS THE FUNCTION OF MUSIC IN DEVISED THEATRE?

It is now generally accepted that all sound can be treated as music, including silence.

Any action on stage will produce a unique sound that potentially can be controlled, amplified, metamorphosed, minimized or ignored; it may help clarify dramatic meaning and intention or undermine the objective. This whole area may then be the joint responsibility of the musical director as well as the director. An early aim in the process might be to raise the awareness of the possibilities within the company by articulating questions, welcoming all answers, and experiencing suggestions through exercises and games in workshops.

WHAT SORT OF MUSIC IS POSSIBLE IN DEVISED THEATRE?

In the early and middle stages of devised theatre, it may be the musical director's responsibility to remind others that any choices made will have a profound effect on the language of the work as a whole. For instance, costumes may themselves be the source of sounds, either deliberately or accidentally. See Chapters 2 and 7 for more ideas on how, by working closely together prior to and during rehearsals, composers and designers can achieve results otherwise unattainable

Conversely, any decision made about instruments will have an effect on the design of the show; instruments carry with them visual and aural associations of history and culture, as well as materials and industrial processing that may or may not be appropriate, and certainly influence the design concept. Musical instruments may also be integrated into the stage design itself.

The table below shows that everything is possible in the relationship between music and drama, along an infinite curve between

Raising Possibilities

It is the director who is responsible for ensuring that the show is a coherent aesthetic whole by the opening night – see Chapter 1. However this may be achieved in endless ways and the composer or designers often make vital and crucial contributions during the process. Also see Chapters 2, 6 and 7.

It will be seen that, because of the potentially ubiquitous nature of music in the theatre, the relationship between the director and the musical director may be crucial: any pre-production research, the amount of music in the show, the sort of music to be used, as well as budgetary considerations and many other questions, hinge on this relationship. But, in devised theatre, the fluidity of the process of creation will be enhanced by delaying the answers to these questions, and allowing the material to suggest itself, rather than be imposed arbitrarily.

	Integration				Separation
Space	No discernible or visible division between actors, singers and instrumentalists: all is fluid movement	Some band players move at certain times to take part in the action, or some singers move to the band area	Singers and actors on stage, band off-stage	Band visible on-stage but to one side, or raised on the set	Band and singers invisible in pit or off-stage
Time	No discernible stopping action to sing, but the music symbiotic with the text; both seemless and fluid	Plays by Beckett, where the sound world is controlled musically by the actor's voice and text	Traditional musical structure of dialogue, underscoring and numbers, e.g. musical *Cabaret*, *West Side Story*	Stylized cutting between dialogue and song	Fixed recorded music dictating length and speed of activities on stage

The role of music in theatre.

An outdoor set which includes large suspended sheets of metal used as instruments, carries great visual power. Grimm Tales. *Salisbury Playhouse/WCYT. August 2000. Written by Carol Ann Duffy. Director: Kirstie Davis. Musical director: Paul Barker. Designer: Alex Eales.* Photo: Alex Eales

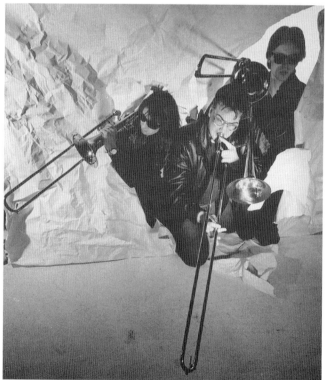

Instruments on stage may develop other characteristics, as in these examples where the guards at the Berlin Wall replace their weaponry with trombones. Wall – Music Theatre by Paul Barker, Modern Music Theatre. Troupe London International Opera Festival 1990.
Photo: Coneyl Jay

symbiosis and autocracy. No single solution or choice is necessarily better than another, and perhaps many different solutions may be employed at different times in the same show, varying the audience's expectations. A completely stylized production will demonstrate a more purist approach, adopting a single relationship and exploring it profoundly.

Everything in theatre has a potential musical effect or consideration. A costume perfect for dancing might restrict the breathing of a singer, while a mask perfect for a role might preclude the possibility of singing. A piece of stage machinery might produce an unintentional sound that interrupts the objective of magic or a crinoline dress may produce such a volume of 'swish' as to be heard as music in itself. Shoes, lighting rigs, faders, mains hum, actors walking and running, unsecured snare drums, external street sounds, nature itself may all have to be considered as allies or foes, as part of the soundscape or a threat to it. Given the infinite variations possible, it sometimes may seem very unimaginative to assign music to a place in a pit beneath the stage.

SHOULD THE PROJECT EMPLOY DEDICATED MUSICIANS?

This is not merely a budgetary consideration, but one that may affect the ethos of the company. If the objective of devised theatre is to create a homogenous, creative company, barriers between session musicians and company members may create a divisive atmosphere. The mere presence of professional musicians may inhibit or inspire the rest of the company in their quest for musical expression. The options are:

- to employ musicians separately;

- to employ musicians with or without a composer among them;
- to recruit musicians from the actors by audition;
- to utilize an open-door policy for rehearsals and to discover and develop whatever skills and abilities are uncovered during the process of devising and creating, as long as there is a strong musical director among the company leaders;
- to use recorded music.

The use of live music always adds life and more layers of communication to the theatre, and energizes performers, permitting an actor's sense of discipline to develop. Actors, on the other hand, stimulate the imagination of musicians beyond the tacitly accepted limits of their musical style. The use of recorded music often has an effect of anaesthetizing the audience's sensitivity – it is always an intrusion from the outside world, cutting through the magic walls of the imagination.

WHAT CAN BE USED TO MAKE MUSIC?

Since everything is possible, no list can be exhaustive. It is useful to categorize the nature of the sound in various groups, according to their origins:

- **Voices:** speaking, chanting, rapping, incantation, whispering alone or in groups, languages, sound versus sense, rhythm and tone in speech, poetic metre, cheering, praying, crowd sounds, dialogue, monologue, vocalisation of sounds, made up languages, idioms, dialects, vernacular, slang, coughing, screaming, diaphragmatic implosions, raspberries, tongue-clicks, rapid ranting;
- **Body sounds:** arm-pits, clapping on various parts of body, stamping, rubbing, whistling,

A collection of instruments designed and constructed for an instrumental and vocal chorus in a recreation of a Noh play, The Fulling Block, *or* Kinuta, *by Zeami, Noh Theatre at Royal Academy of Dramatic Art, 1998. Director: William Gaskill Composer: Paul Barker. Photo: Henk Schut*

squeaking, breathing, eyelids closing and opening, walking, running, finger-clicks, jumping.

- **Home-made instruments:** bottles, boxes, plastic containers, tearing cloth or paper, elastic bands, comb and brown paper, sand or beans in a container, recycled parts of cars or machinery, plastic bags, balloons (pitched and popping), whips, claves, bells, pots and pans, suspended metal sheets, wine glass rubbing.
- **Found 'natural' instruments:** stones, logs (especially hollow), sticks, sand, tiny pebbles, large pebbles, dried beans in containers.

The Importance of Reliable Percussion Sticks or Mallets

These tools can be an art in themselves, and it may be worth considering spending some of the budget eventually in buying or professionally hiring them. The real thing is both durable and efficient.

A certain scene is being worked on. Divide the company into several groups to simultaneously create their appropriate music to the scene. Questions should be asked and individual answers sought, for example:

- How can musical instruments be incorporated into the performance and design? (For more information on design ideas and suggestions see Chapters 3, 2 and 7.)
- What is the purpose of music in the scene?
- Will it add something beyond the text and action?
- Where will the music come from, outside the action, or from within?

In working on the scene, different groups will employ different skills: some may have instruments, others voices, or a mixture of both. The actors themselves may be a part of one group or divided among several, which might emphasize an organic nature to the music, rather than imposing it from the outside. At the end of a given rehearsal period, during which time the musical director circulates, catalyses and encourages the process, the whole company gather to view, hear and discuss the results. Often there are good ideas in more than one group, in which case a decision is made to create an amalgam of all the best ideas. By reshuffling the groups into a repetition of the process, with the best of the shared material, people forget where the original ideas come from, and the music seems to grow from the company, rather than through any one individual.

It is important to emphasize that the de-selection of material is just as important as the selection. The company eventually defines what the end material will be by rejecting a mass of other material, and in that way the identity of the work gradually becomes clear. It is not a failure of creativity, but an important defining moment, which otherwise could not be articulated. Understanding what does not work and why, helps us to understand what does. Early danger signs are when an individual (company leader or member) has an idea that they will not let go, and sees the acceptance or rejection of their idea as a personal statement. The process of devising is more akin to sculpture: what is rejected and what is eventually disclosed underneath, define the end result.

Sometimes, as a musical director, you may be asked to supply music as an entr'acte, or in order to cover some stage machinery or even backstage business. This might seem to be an unnecessary weakening of the structure of the work, and a misuse of the value of music. In devised theatre, above all, there might seem to be little need for this, since the performers and creators have full authority. Do not be afraid to say so!

How Can a Song be Devised?

Often in a devised work, there will be the need for a song. The process of devising a song in a company replicates in a microcosm the process of musical devising in the theatre, and bears a direct relation to the process of devising drama. There are many ways to do it, but the one outlined here is one that allows for the maximum collaboration and variation of outcome. The length of this process will depend upon the number of people involved, but should ideally cover several rehearsal sessions. It does take time to create music, and this process should not be rushed the first time. However, on subsequent song workshops, time limits of five or ten minutes for each section may aid the delivery. A little adrenaline aids the process.

Step One

The text should be devised. If there are individuals in the company who either speak another language, or for whom English is not their first language, here is a good opportunity to enrich the cultural backdrop of the work.

After discussing the dramatic function of the song, some key words should be collected. Working in small groups of three or four, several attempts can be made for verses or choruses to be presented verbally for all to discuss. On the whole, people always write too many words when trying to write a song; some really excellent songs have only one or two lines. Find some models that you like, and follow this thought through with the company.

Step Two

Eventually, a short set of words is selected by all. At this point, you should introduce a rule, which is really a guideline. It is no secret (although you might introduce it as such) that almost all great songs follow this rule: important words are always set higher and last longer than unimportant words.

Again, working in small groups, tell them to assign each word a number 1–5, with 1 as the most important. Some words will be polysyllabic, and each syllable should be labelled i, ii, iii, etc., with i as the most important. It is crucial at this stage to demonstrate that what may be important to someone, may be less so to another. Individuals should be encouraged to offer different solutions, as there is no absolute right or wrong answer here. The process is personal, subjective and shows valid, different ways of interpreting the same text.

Prompt Point

For more exercises designed both to produce performance material and build group confidence see Chapters 3, 6 and 1.

Step Three

After everyone has created their own numbering system, it may be a good idea to draw a simple line-graph with relative pitch and time above the text. Each person must then speak the text on their own, following the ups and downs shown by the hierarchical numbers. This might be best done with everyone in the same room at the same time, as the background of noise will help everyone's confidence. Their objective is to find a shape that pleases, and adds something to the text when spoken normally. (It is assumed that by this stage some preliminary work has been done sensitizing the company's understanding of pitch in relation to the spoken voice.)

Step Four

Now exaggerate the spoken version, using as much of each individual's own vocal range as possible. (We also assume here that some prior work-shopping has taken place in vocal production.) The first objective is to exaggerate beyond what is tasteful or deemed appropriate. Once that limit has been found, it may be necessary to tame the exaggeration, but only a little. Generally people find they are restricted by their inhibitions and need to discover the joy of taking risks. The second objective is to choose something that can be repeated, to some extent.

Step Five

Go to an instrument (or work in pairs with at least one person who has one) and try and find some of the notes you have been working on that work with your voice. Since memory is being tested here, it is probably better that everyone is working on just half a dozen words or so, because eventually, each person has to perform for a few seconds to the others in the group after an agreed time. A tape-recorder

An exciting moment of improvisation reached by three dancers provoked by the natural light in the rehearsal space and music. Julie Blackman and dancers in rehearsal improvising to music and light. Photo: Tony Nandi

might help at this stage, as you can take each individual out of the room and record their offering, without interrupting the process or concentration.

Step Six

After listening to the recordings, the group discusses and chooses what goes forward for more development. The eventual song may turn out to be a smoothly constructed patchwork of the chosen ideas.

DOES THE MUSIC ALWAYS COME SECOND?

Sometimes music can be the starting point for a dramatic exercise. If the composition of music always comes after text or movement, an important aspect between it and the other performing arts may be ignored, and the place of music relegated unnecessarily.

SHOULD THE SCORE FOR THE SHOW BE WRITTEN DOWN?

The more that can be recorded in this way, the better. There are two reasons for writing a score for theatre: to remember what happens from one rehearsal to the next, and to remember what happens musically in the production. Whether the score utilizes traditional musical notation or not only relates to the performers' abilities. A musical score is only a memory aid. Whether graphics, shorthand or staves are used, whatever language the music is written in, it would be a good idea if the stage manager on the book (as it evolves) has some working knowledge of it.

HOW BIG SHOULD A WORKING GROUP BE IN THIS KIND OF REHEARSAL?

Big enough to give confidence to those lacking it, but not so big that people can hide behind the group. Everyone should be able to communicate freely, so start with three to five people. As the company increases its experience and trust, the groups can become bigger. Everyone should be in a position to feel confident about articulating and vocalizing their thoughts, without fear of ridicule of failure.

Ultimately, everyone should be encouraged to be involved in musical creation and performance. It is always a good idea to start with that objective and hold on to it as long as possible, as the alternative may be to change one ethos of what devised theatre is about. As ever, the end product may need a compromise somewhere in order to maintain a control over quality. This is a responsibility of the musical director. If the morale of the company is well-developed and nurtured in the early stages, this sort of compromise at a later stage will not be too difficult for them to assimilate.

WHAT IS THE PLACE OF SOUND-EFFECTS?

Recording melons being punched, cauliflowers being chopped or steam-train whistles blowing may seem creative and imaginative alternatives to real on-stage violence or expensive sets, but music is a language in itself: it has its own objectives and also amplifies the theatrical language. To see a punch on stage may be enough without hearing it, too. Audiences are really quite sophisticated and they may recognize that a bit of smoke and a recording of a train whistle remain just that, and, worse, may be reminded through them of the limitations of theatre, rather than any magic. Sound-effects as such are only a decoration and often simply repeat imagery or language. Music, on the other hand, has the ability to communicate something beyond the visual or textual domain. Sound-effects, on the other hand, when treated as music and used structurally or developmentally, cease to be merely sound-effects. The train whistle that discloses a lover's whispered endearment may do just that after several hearings.

WHAT BUDGETARY CONSIDERATIONS ARE THERE?

Music contributes to every area of theatre, and the budget should be proportional to that relationship. Instruments may need to be hired, bought or created and even redesigned or visually disguised. If recordings or amplification are used, the amount paid for the equipment usually reflects the value of the sound given to the product. Music can be expensive – instruments, equipment, studio time, etc. – devised theatre that is about human resources is also about human resourcefulness. A set that incorporates instruments and actors who think of themselves as musicians may be an alternative to agreeing a purely musical budget beforehand. The director and producer need to know as much as possible about the financial repercussions of decisions as soon as possible (see Chapters 1 and 9).

HOW DO YOU CROSS THE SINGING BARRIER THAT SO MANY PERFORMERS HAVE?

Singing is largely a matter of confidence and context. Not everyone can sing numbers from *Cabaret*, for instance, but devised theatre allows material to be created specifically for the individual. The trick is to find what someone can do – speak in time, rap, a range of three notes, create a pure child-like sound, imitate Meatloaf – and create the material around that, in relationship to the work.

The nurturing of the actor's understanding of the voice is a core activity in all theatre, not just devised theatre. It is an area worthy of a whole chapter to itself. As has already been pointed out, much time should be created in the early stages to workshop this crucial area for the whole company. (The development of the multi-skilled performer is essential as explored in Chapters 3 and 6.)

EXERCISES

Aim to improve everyone's skill strengths, and to acknowledge and give time to develop their work. Objective: levelling the musical playground:

Exercise 1: Stoneplay – a New View of Rhythm

1. Find some river stones – smooth, dry, palm-size and strong. The best are found on beaches, but beware that removing them may be illegal! Rivers and garden centres are good alternative sources.
2. Explore the stones as a source for sound: rubbing, tapping together (different according to how they are held), dropping, slapping, banging on the floor, rolling, etc., all produce different sounds. The more sensitive will discover these actions produce related smells from the stones!
3. Place them in the palm of your hands and play them by striking together. Notice how the sound changes according to how they are held and struck. One person leads the circle, and all try to play at exactly the same time. Or the objective is to catch the others out. An in-breath is a good way of leading or conducting, which is the essence of the exercise, which must be un-pulsed, without a beat.
4. In a circle, a pulse is established. Each person in turn must improvise a rhythm for eight beats, as interestingly as possible.

(Above and opposite) The use of microphones can add theatricality to the moment. La Pazzia Senile by Banchieri/Chris Newell. Modern Music Theatre Troupe, South Bank Arts Centre, 1994.

5. Improvise two lines of text or dialogue, in pairs. Memorize its sound and then replicate the word-sounds with the stones, as a monologue or a duet. Communicate with the stones.

Exercise 2: Voiceplay – a New View of Pitching

6. All sing one note. The leader must go to each person in turn to show how the physical nature of the sound and its reverberation can be felt. Those with difficulties in hearing pitches can thus be led, by feeling them, to reproduce them.

7. In a circle, all facing clockwise. All hum any note, changing between breaths at will. The person behind explores the body of the person in front, to identify the areas of strongest vibrations. The back, the head, the leg, the foot, the arm, a finger – all should be explored and compared with others' results before turning anti-clockwise to repeat the process. At a second, later stage, the singer must try to activate a vibration in the part of the body that is being touched, and the toucher should not move fingertips until some vibration is felt.

8. Human xylophone: one leader drawn from the group 'plays' by touching or pointing. The human 'keys' articulate gestures, pitches, noises etc, reacting to the changing volume and duration as directed by the leader.

6 MOVEMENT DIRECTION
Ruth Naylor-Smith

Movement directing for devised theatre is exciting and scary because anything can happen. It is demanding and easy because you are asked difficult questions, but you do not have to answer them on your own. It is frustrating and rewarding work because experimentation finally leads to the right results. If you want to movement direct for devised theatre, you have to accept that these contradictions are the rules of the game. This chapter hopes to encourage and help you to play.

The director will define your part within the devising process. He decides whether a movement director is needed and how big an influence they will have on the piece. A movement director can be employed full-time as part of the creative team or sometimes an actor is given the job. The responsibility could be carried by both director and actors, or a specialist could be employed for a short amount of time to do one particular task (teach stilt-walking, choreograph a dance). Whatever the scenario, the process remains similar and it always begins with research.

RESEARCH

The most important research is the study of the source material itself: immerse yourself in it. Look at it first as a punter and enjoy it for what it is. Then work out what is at the heart of the material, the focus point that motors the whole. It could be driven by its story, its characters, its environment, or abstract shapes and sounds. Find out about the environment of the source material. This part of the research can be as varied and as wide as there are source materials available, but you need to know what affects the movement of this world: custom, class, nationality, health, clothes, employment, landscape, music, dance, sport.

Gather pictures and keep notes, because they will be invaluable later. Let your imagination run wild with all the different movement possibilities, but do not become fixated with one idea. Always remember that research is about gathering information, not decision-making.

PRE-PRODUCTION MEETINGS

This is a time for listening, and getting a feel for the project. You will find out what inspired the

---

Prompt Points

The movement director works alongside a whole team to discover the most elegant and interesting performance solutions. Her work is intimately related to the work of the director (Chapter 1) the composer (Chapter 5), the performer (Chapter 3) the designers (Chapters 2 and 7).

production, and the journey those ideas have taken from their conception. Try to sense how stylized the piece will be and if there are underlying themes you can pick up on.

Each department will add more colour to the growing picture in your head. Stay open. A casual suggestion from someone else may spark an inferno of new ideas in your head. Whilst you are jumping up and down in excitement over the latest suggestion, do not forget to be practical. How many specific skills can you realistically expect your cast to cover (actors who can tango, caricature an old woman, play the trumpet and be a sympathetic hero may not be easy to find). It will take time to learn new styles and skills and your cast will need to be comfortable with them before they can use them in devising.

A highly stylized **Romeo and Juliet** *with the principal characters as naive clowns. Photo: Roland Quesnel*

Finding the peak of the music with the composer. Photo: Michael Castleton

Try to understand how other people work. Each department will have its own challenges and deadlines to meet. The composer may wish to create some pieces before rehearsals commence, so agree upon a few places where the music will lead the action (in a dance, for example) and then discuss style, mood and tempo.

Before you start rehearsing, you should have a clear idea of the parameters of the piece. You will not know what the final picture will look like, but you should know what materials you will be using to create it.

Also, see Chapter 8 for the importance of pre-production meetings.

AUDITIONS

In devised theatre an interesting balance of performers is more important than casting for roles. As a movement director you want to find performers who are comfortable with their physicality, able to use their whole body sensitively, and who are eager to respond openly. Agree beforehand with the director the basic level of movement skill required.

The director and producer and performer all have different perspectives on auditions (see Chapters 1, 3 and 9 for more details).

Casting Pitfalls

Avoid someone who impresses but wants

to be the star all the time – there is no room for huge egos in devising. Do not get side tracked by someone's speciality – an acrobat will not be useful in a naturalistic drama. Be wary of over-concentrating on a skill for one potential scene (a tap dance). The scene may not make the final performance, the actors will.

PLANNING REHEARSALS

The director is ultimately responsible for the production, as they have to ensure the piece works as a whole. It is imperative that you work together. Your job is to physically realize the piece, to use your skills to enhance the director's ideas, sometimes fine-tuning what is already there and at other times opening up different movement possibilities. Together you need to plan each session, decide who is leading and at what point the other gets involved or takes over.

Typical Structure of a Session

- Warm up; make sure the performers are physically and mentally prepared.
- Play a game; ensure that all are relaxed and responding spontaneously.
- Exercises; establish the style or physical language you will be working in.
- Improvisations or set tasks; set up a structure within which the performers can play and experiment. Enable them to make their own discoveries within the physical language.

Actors playing Pulling Faces before a dress rehearsal. Photo: Ruth Naylor-Smith

- Discussions; analyse discoveries and agree on their best application to the piece.
- Work directly on the piece; look at scenes that will benefit from the new physical language.

EARLY REHEARSALS

Time to play. At last the talking is over and the action can commence; it is time to get the piece moving. The first step is to give your cast the confidence to express themselves physically. When a performer meets a movement director, a typical response is 'I'm not very good at movement'. You have to disprove this statement by accepting them as they are and encouraging them to use what they have. Begin with games that encourage physical spontaneity(see Exercises). Join in and have some fun (if you are, everyone else can too). Zip, Zap, Biong (Exercise 2) is good because you do not have time to think before sending a clap onwards. Pulling faces forces everyone to leave their self-image behind. As the game progresses the face and its attitude start to take over the whole body. This usually happens without any prompting, as people begin to respond with their subconscious.

At all times accept and encourage. Allow the cast the freedom to play. Once your cast is ready to play, you can begin. But where do you start? In scripted work you are given your story, characters, settings and sometimes even stage directions. The challenges are laid out in front of you. In devised work it is less clear. It is like being given a blank piece of paper. It is up to you to hand out the crayons that enable the cast to draw.

Begin with what you have – your source material and your research. Whatever you decided was the driving force of the source material will drive the devising process. If the material is driven by a story, ask the cast to tell you that story in six pictures. Then ask them to act out the story without any words. Both of these exercises require preparation and get the cast discussing the material from a physical angle. Watch what has been created and note where action best conveys the story and when it leaves issues unclear. Observe how the cast differentiate characters, how they create spaces and move from one to another. Discuss what you have discovered with the cast, director and writer.

Characters are usually important in devised work as their wants and needs motivate new discoveries. There are numerous ways of creating characters physically and each way can leave its stamp upon the production. Most actors have an unconscious list of characters that they always play, so it is a good idea to give them a fresh impulse. Different stimuli include:

- the factual (how people really move) created by observation, costume and re-enactments of physical activities;
- the picture (any picture, painting, cartoon or sculpture): copy the stance and attitude of the character to give you a starting point from which to invent;
- the abstract (starting from an animal, colour, material, element, music, emotion, etc.): exploring the attitude and dynamics of the abstract and then retaining them in human form (see Exercises);
- the details (allowing one small physical detail affect the rest of the body): pick a part of the body that always leads (nose, stomach), or concentrate on bandy legs, or shy hands;
- the mask or puppet, which can become the focus of the performer and thus take over their body.

Allow the cast time to familiarize themselves with the general physical style before they concentrate on their own roles. If they are multi-role playing, they can use the style to

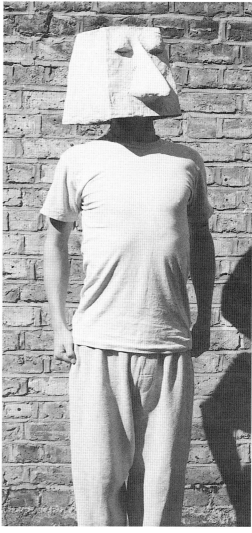

An actor's physicality changes in response to two contrasting masks.
Photo: Ruth Naylor-Smith

change character from water to fire, nose-led to groin-led, peasant to landlord. If you know you need a group of opposing people, one way in would be to begin with materials that react strongly to each other. Let the cast play with different ideas and stress that this is only a starting point. It is vitally important that the characters are given the freedom to live. The truth of the character will come from the commitment of the performer, so allow the performer the chance to experiment and make discoveries for themselves.

The environment of the source material is vitally important. Share your research with the cast and find a way of enabling them to experience the environment. You can take your cast to different places by using whatever you have in the rehearsal room to recreate the space. Ask them to close their eyes while you describe the imagined space to them and then tell them to open their eyes to see and be in the imagined space. Ask everyone to visit the space one by one, building upon each others' observations. You can ask each cast member to take you on a journey to see the space; you can use music, sound, lights, smells to help. What is important is that the cast feel and understand the environment and its atmosphere and that they recognize how their physicality is affected.

Different spaces and atmospheres are clearly reflected in the body. On an empty stage you can tell whether someone is sitting at home or in a strange place, purely by their physicality (see diagram).

When your cast know the physicality of an environment, you can use it as a stimulus for devising. Set up an improvisation that concentrates on the environment and then begin to play with the shapes, rhythms, focus, tension levels of the improvisation. Take a market place and improvise a short scene, concentrating on the reality of the movement. Then ask everyone to move more quickly, double their tension level, acknowledge one person of their choice, avoid another and get something from a third. Suddenly you will have an interesting and dynamic scene with lots of potential stories emerging. Take a three-person lift with five people in it. Again create the reality of the scene. Then move the actors into a space on their own and ask them to re-enact the scene. The observer will become more interested in the individuals and the style of the piece will have moved from the naturalistic to the abstract.

Creating Space On-Stage

How you choose to recreate a space on stage will have a huge effect on the style of the production. To make such decisions you need the help of the other departments. For example, let us imagine that a car is a vital ingredient of the piece. There are eight (or more) ways to create a car, and they demand the involvement of different people:

- a real car – set designer;
- parts of a car – set or costume designer, movement director;
- bodies making a car – movement director;
- miming the use of a car – movement director;
- chairs and outline of car drawn in the air – set designer, movement director;
- a puppet car – set or costume designer, movement director;
- a car that is seen and described – movement director, writer;
- a car that is a lighting effect – set and lighting designers.

All the above would be aided by sound effects. A variation of this list would apply equally well to the creation of a saloon, a desert, a tea pot. To find out which solution best suits your production (and its budget) try the most appropriate ones.

As the rehearsal process continues, do not forget the rest of the production team. If the tap routine has been cut, tell the costume department! If your stage manager is in the rehearsal room they will make notes of these things, but do not expect them to be superhuman. At the end of a session, have a natter with them and the director, to clarify what decisions have been made and what actions need to be taken.

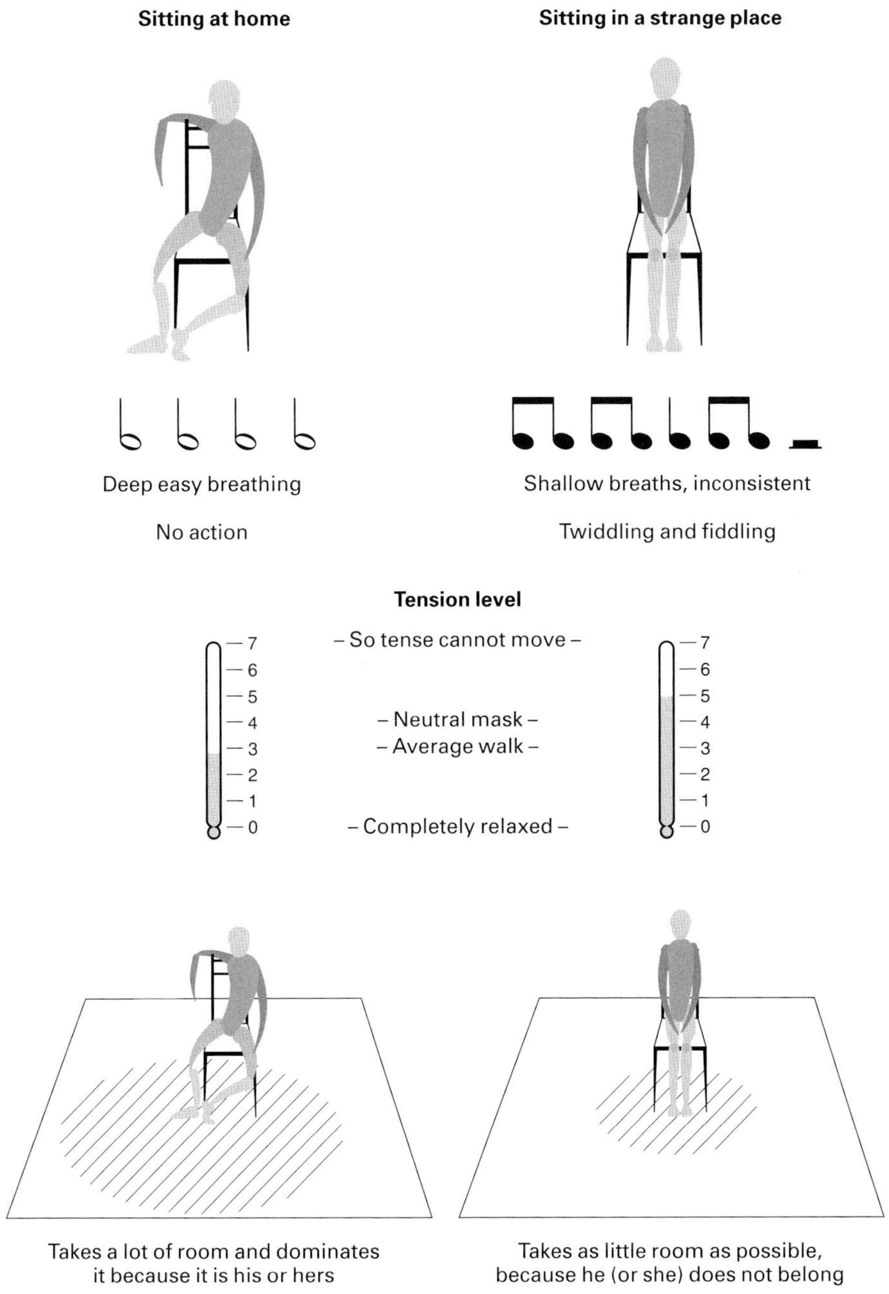

Sitting at home

Sitting in a strange place

Deep easy breathing

Shallow breaths, inconsistent

No action

Twiddling and fiddling

Tension level

– So tense cannot move –

– Neutral mask –
– Average walk –

– Completely relaxed –

Takes a lot of room and dominates
it because it is his or hers

Takes as little room as possible,
because he (or she) does not belong

How the body responds to two different spaces. Their body will also influence what happens next; one could doze off, the other could not.

95

'Let's try it'

This is an important phrase in devised theatre. If you try it, you will know if it works. Hours can be wasted indulging in hypothetical discussions, especially if you reach a difficult scene and energy levels are low. Sometimes it is a good idea to challenge the cast to find three ways of solving the problem, rather than the best way, as it relieves the pressure.

Gather as many bits of costume and props (or mock-ups) as possible, for these will fuel the creative process. Let the relevant designer know when you will be playing with their creation. They can explain how they imagined it moving, the actor can then experiment, you and the designer can throw in ideas. Inanimate objects can only live and work when the performers believe in them, so do ensure that the actor has the time and space to own the costume, prop, puppet, mask, and play with it in a focused environment. After experimentation and an open discussion, any necessary adaptations can be made. Everyone understands why the initial idea must change and how they can help to make the new idea work.

A similar process must be worked through with the composer, who will have created the music with a shape and feel in mind. Make sure you soak up everything that is in the music before you get tied down with detailed choreography. This may involve asking

Trying to inspire when the energy level has dropped. Photo: Hannah Bicât

These characters came from a collaboration between movement director, costume designer and actors. Photo: Roland Quesnel

everyone to lie down and listen with their eyes closed, or having the group up on their feet so they can wiggle with freedom. You should be aiming to fit your choreography perfectly to the music, but always find out how difficult it would be to make alterations.

If the piece of music is to be action-led, you will need to show the composer your choreography. Make sure that it is performed with commitment, so the atmosphere as well as the moves are clear. The composer will probably want to take over the session then, so take a back seat and let them play around with what they see. It may be that changing certain moves and personnel, or altering some timings, will greatly enhance the musical interpretation – so be ready to adapt.

Dangerous Moves

Do not be reticent about setting the odd move early on. An acrobatic lift or a precisely timed piece of choreography will need to be practised. Be firm about this if you need to be. Remember it is easier to cut than to add a difficult move.

A lovely image that required much practice. Photo: Roland Quesnel

LATER REHEARSALS

If the early part of rehearsals is primarily about initiating, the latter part is about responding. By now every one should be comfortable with the physical language of the production and be freely inventing within it.

You need to spot ideas that could be pushed, images that could be strengthened, timings that could be tightened. Basically the piece and the performers become the stimulus from which you create.

Later rehearsals tend to be more fluid than

98

The central character is approached from all sides creating a strong shape and intimidating dynamic. Photo: Malachi Bogdanov

Do Not Panic

At least once during the rehearsal process someone will come up with an idea that you are totally unprepared for; 'a balletic *pas de deux* would be perfect here'. Ask what qualities make it right, is it the harmony, the elegance, the fact that the man is lifting the woman? Put people into pairs and ask them to come up with an image for each of the above. You should now have enough material to play with.

the early ones and it can be harder to judge when your input would help. Be clear about who is in charge of each session (usually the director) and refer to them. Even when your brain is bursting with ideas, let the director finish what he or she wants to accomplish and then jump in. Premature inputs can disrupt the flow and result in chaos. Well-timed ideas bring scenes to life.

By this stage the general shape and style of the production should be established. Sections that do not fit any more will need to be altered or cut. This requires a brutal approach, as you may need to lose a favourite moment for the good of the piece as a whole. It is also time to be clear about what is set and what is to be improvised during performances. Knowing when definitively to set a scene is a tricky judgement call in devised work.

As everyone has been used to the excitement of playing and discovering, repeating and finalizing can seem incredibly dull and it is common for the cast to lose confidence in the material. But, in order for some physical routines to work well every night in front of a live audience, you need to rehearse them. You may have to bully your cast through the repetitious stage, reassuring them that the joy of playing will return once the details are so familiar that they do not need to think of them any more.

TECHNICAL AND DRESS REHEARSALS

Encourage your cast to use these rehearsals to really explore the stage, set, costume, lighting design. They need to feel comfortable in their surroundings, so that they can move with freedom and confidence. They have created the piece, now they have to make it live for others. It is time to play with an audience.

Checklist

Research:
- know your source material well and study its environment;
- look for the driving force of the material.

Pre-production meetings:
- listen, get a feel for the direction of the piece;
- understand how others work.

Auditions:
- look for versatile, responsive, physically sensitive performers.

Rehearsals:
- be clear about who is leading and plan sessions in advance;
- develop trust, respect and confidence;
- establish a movement language early so ideas come from the same base;
- teach new skills. empower the actors;
- keep communicating with the production team and give them the space and time to make their creations work;
- try it; discoveries are made faster through doing;
- set difficult moves early, they will need to be practised;
- ensure the piece works as a whole and cut or adapt accordingly;
- practise and tweak.

EXERCISES

Exercise 1: Keep the Ball Up

1. Find a medium-sized soft ball and keep it in the air for as long as you can. You are not allowed to touch the ball twice in succession. Work as a team.
2. When you have mastered this try 'fives'. Exactly the same rules except that every fifth touch must be with a part of the body other than the hand (head, knee, foot, shoulder, elbow).

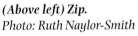

(Above left) Zip.
Photo: Ruth Naylor-Smith

(Above right) Boing.
Photo: Ruth Naylor-Smith

Exercise 2: Zip Zap Boing

1. Stand in a circle.
2. Pass a clap around the circle as fast as you can (you clap to your right, then the person on your right claps to their right and so on) This is called a zip.
3. Block the zip and send it back in the opposite direction with a boing. Clap the hands together and then put them out in front of you as if you were pushing someone away.
4. Practice zipping and boinging.
5. Add zapping. To zap clap your hands together and point them very directly at someone in the circle (not the person on your left or right). Make good eye contact with them.
6. Zip zap and boing as quickly as you can, using the body, arms and eyes to direct the clap. Enjoy the rhythms that emerge.

101

Exercise 3: Pulling Faces

Stand in a circle.

1. A pulls a silly face at the others in the circle.
2. A looks at the person on their left (B) and gives them the face.
3. B copies the face and the spirit behind it.
4. A relaxes once (B) has got the face.
5. B looks at the others in the circle and changes the face.
6. B looks at the person on their left (C) who copies the face...
7. And so on around the circle.

As the game progresses, the attitude of the face will usually begin to take over the whole body. Then people start to move a little, then they may go for a short wander. All these things are to be encouraged without ever letting the energy drop.

If you can sense that people are pre-planning their faces, persuade them to have a go at letting their faces evolve from the previous face. Do not think, do. You can also try zapping the faces across the circle to break the routine and surprise people.

Fully committed, playful movement from pulling a silly face. Photo: Ruth Naylor-Smith

Exercise 4: Individual Movement Routine

This is a demanding, but revealing audition exercise.

Suggested movements:

- close to open;
- arm swings;
- look and lunge;
- undulation;
- acrobatic free choice (cartwheel);
- turn;
- balance;
- run and jump.

1. Teach everyone the routine. Demonstrate fully and correct misunderstandings. Give people time to practise and be available to answer questions. Stress that you are looking for a controlled and rhythmic performance that is true to the movement routine.

2. See the routines individually or in groups, depending on time, space, and so on. You are looking for people who are centred and comfortable in their body, who have a strong neutral stage presence and are willing to let the movements speak for themselves.

1. Closed to open

Use the most direct route.
Take the space

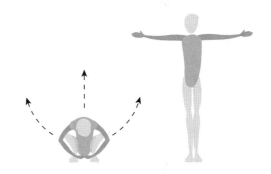

2. Arm swings (×4)

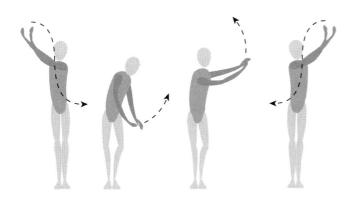

Use the weight of the arms to let them swing easily. In a figure of eight pattern.

Individual movement routine.

3. Look and lunge

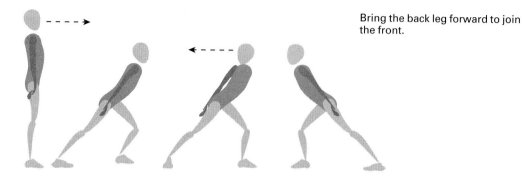

Bring the back leg forward to join the front.

4. Undulation

This is a fluid movement. Let the arms hang at ease by the side.

5. Free choice; something acrobatic
Foreward roll, cartwheel, handstand, etc.

6. Turn on one leg

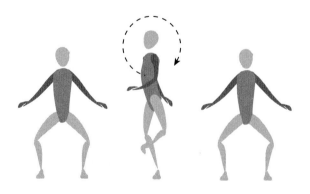

Shift your balance onto the supporting leg whilst pushing off with the other leg to do a full spin (360°).

7. Balance

Hold the balance until you are stable.

8. Run and jump

3. Now see what they can do with the routine themselves. Ask them to retain the basic movements and the given order of the piece, but to explode everything else with their own ideas. They may like to play with the rhythms and textures of the movements, reverse the undulation, add tap shuffles to the run, do triple spins. They might like to add character or atmosphere to the piece, e.g. a cat-like human being chased. The routine could symbolize something. Stress that anything is possible and that it is a chance to play and show what they can do. (If you have only two or three people auditioning, you might like to leave the room for five minutes so that they can play without being self conscious. In large groups this is not a problem.)

4. Finally the new creative routines.

Exercise 5: Finding Characters and Exploring Levels of Stylization

Begin with something abstract or non-human – this could be a colour, material, animal, emotion, element, etc.

1. Ask everyone to lie down, close their eyes and picture their abstraction. See how it moves. Recognize how it feels. Then breathe in the attitude of their abstraction.

2. Ask them to get themselves into a position that suits their abstraction.

3. When they are ready they may open their eyes and begin to move. When their eyes open, the attitude of the abstraction must be there.

4. Explore in detail the extreme abstraction. How does it move? Is it fast/slow, direct/indirect, smooth/jerky, how heavy or light, tense or relaxed, does it dominate the space or skirt around it, what is its rhythm? Most importantly what is its attitude?

5. Allow time for exploration. Interject questions or suggestions to stimulate, but do not make direct contact.

6. When the time is right, draw the exercise to a close.

7. Discuss the different movement qualities that have been discovered. Comment on the most powerful images, and stress the importance of the attitude underpinning everything.

8. Explain that what they have just done was level number ten, as abstract as possible. Level number one is as human/naturalistic as possible, whilst retaining the same attitude and movement qualities. Say that you will now count from ten to one and you would like them to hit each level with you.

9. Ask them to close their eyes, take a few deep breaths, and then revisit that level number ten.

10. Gradually count down stressing the half-way point, etc. As they become more human you might suggest some naturalistic actions like sitting, lying, looking at a book.

11. When you have gone from ten to one jump around the levels a bit. You might like to ask everyone to become aware of the other people in the room, and see how they interact at the different levels.

12. Finally discuss what has been experienced and observed, and relate it to your piece.

This exercise can be done in reverse, starting with a naturalistic character and pushing certain elements through the levels to caricature and abstraction.

From old lady, to caricature, to abstract.

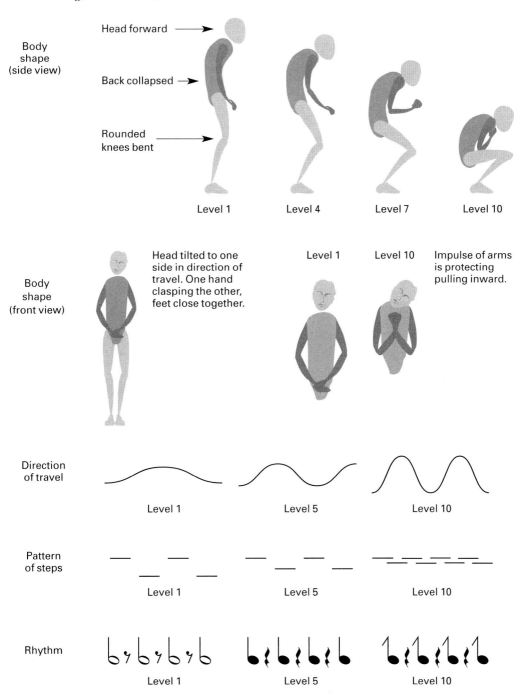

Body shape (side view)

Head forward →

Back collapsed →

Rounded knees bent →

Level 1   Level 4   Level 7   Level 10

Body shape (front view)

Head tilted to one side in direction of travel. One hand clasping the other, feet close together.

Level 1   Level 10   Impulse of arms is protecting pulling inward.

Direction of travel

Level 1   Level 5   Level 10

Pattern of steps

Level 1   Level 5   Level 10

Rhythm

Level 1   Level 5   Level 10

107

7 DESIGNING AND MAKING COSTUMES

Tina Bicât

Costumes for devised theatre cannot be designed and made in advance but must be created as the work grows. Although this can be a frightening way to work, it is possible to create the most exciting effects, and to give the actors extraordinary ease and pleasure in a costume created for their particular realization of a role. This ease is even more marked when the design for the costume has been conceived and grown after discussion sparked by their own work. The confidence in the information given out by their appearance gives daring and depth to the message they give to the audience.

More often than not a devised production is created in a short rehearsal time and on a smallish budget. The company must have freedom to try out their ideas and it is necessary to provide a strict framework within which ideas may flow freely but not become impossible to realize. The workload and its cost can easily spiral into complete chaos, and the devising costumier will find herself with a massive and impossible list of costumes to complete in the last few days. The ideas may be there, but they may disappear in the lurking, fatal pitfalls of no time and no money.

Every play has its particular needs. The following suggestions take a costume designer or maker through a project and are followed by a checklist, which sums up the points discussed. More particular information for the actual design and making of costumes can be found in the bibliography.

RESEARCH

As soon as you know you are going to design or make costumes for a production, ideas and pictures will start rushing into your head. It is surprisingly easy to get hooked onto an inappropriate idea and, also, surprisingly hard to unhook yourself; most particularly when there is no script to give a pathway for your thoughts. The object of research is to make sure that the costume conjured up is appropriate. The wider and more thorough your research, the more likely you are to make a good job of it.

Make yourself familiar with the theme of the production as early as possible. Talk to the director and writer, and try to understand their ideas. Ask questions, share your thoughts and above all listen, to catch the feeling and spirit of their idea, as well as its content. Discover the route that has led them to the project; it may prove a valuable route for your better understanding of the thoughts hidden in their hearts and heads. Your costumes must reflect these thoughts.

If the work is based on a novel or a story, read it often until you know the characters and

Final design for a costume built up through discussion and rehearsals on a base of corset and petticoat. (Left) The design. (Right) The completed costume. Photo: Robin Cottrell

Changes to the script being proposed during a break in rehearsal.
Photo: Hannah Bicât

can imagine the way they live. Study the period so that you have a clear picture of the clothes that were worn by different classes and on different occasions. Read how people thought and the way they and their families spent their days. And those ever-changing mysteries of class and etiquette must be absorbed into your store of knowledge. It is not enough just to look up apt fashions in a costume book: you are trying to understand the people as well as their clothes.

Research may take you to zoos and stations, hospitals and playgrounds, as well as to libraries and museums. And very little beats chatting to someone who was there. Devised work can range far and wide – your research must also range far and wide, if it is to be useful. You cannot foretell what knowledge you will need: research fills your larder – it is your supplies. You will not need all of it, but it will be ready for you to grab in a hurry, or for anyone else in the rehearsal room to grab, when it is wanted. At all discussions you should be able to approach the work from an informed and generous perspective.

Prompt Point

Research is crucial, as all chapters point out. For the costume designer it is essential to keep in close communication with the director (Chapter 1), movement director (Chapter 6) and the set designer (Chapter 2). And is the composer really thinking of using trombones instead of guns for the soldiers? (see Chapter 5).

PRE-PRODUCTION DISCUSSIONS

Try to arrive at the first meeting with an open mind – this requires the self-control of a crocodile trying not to bite the delicious baby in its jaws – but try. It is most important that your research should not lead you to an unshakeable decision before you have conferred with the rest of the company.

The costume department has a double aim in these discussions. The first is, like all the

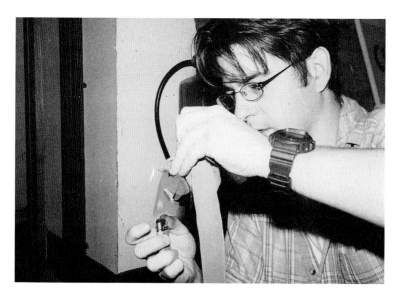

Balancing invention and practicality – in this case testing whether the cloth for the wings of a bird costume is fireproof. Photo: *Tina Bicât*

Different aspects of a production being discussed in rehearsal. Photo: Tina Bicât

other departments, to get a feeling of the way the work will cook – devised work can use so many different ingredients – and, of course, to get to know the rest of the crew and learn to understand their vocabulary of ideas. The original idea for the work may spring from a story, perhaps a novel or a fairy tale; there may be a particular political or social event or argument; or something much more abstract. As a costume designer, you will need to gauge the degree of reality in your costumes to fit with the style of production. This sounds a tall order so early in the proceedings, but it is easier than it sounds. The way the director and/or writer talks about ideas and rehearsal practice at pre-production discussions will point you in the right way. You will need to exchange ideas with the set designer to make sure your ideas

coincide. A detailed discussion between the movement director and stage manager, for instance, may not concern you directly – but listen. Every exchange of ideas will help you to a better understanding of the way your co-workers think and the vocabulary they use to explain their thoughts.

The second aim is entirely practical and will prove unnecessary if you have a generous budget and a long rehearsal period: it is to ascertain what work, apart from research, you can do before the rush of rehearsal. You can never be sure what costumes and accessories will prove essential, but you can make a good guess. When rehearsal time is short and money limited, it may actually help the actors to have a rough picture of the way they will be dressed. In pre-production discussion you have to begin the process, which will be with you throughout the whole project, of balancing invention with practicality.

It is also vital in these pre-production discussions to address that most essential subject: the budget.

The Budget

Allocating the budget is a balancing task for the devising costumier. On one side lies extravagant enthusiasm and running out of money, and on the other overcautious thrift and an unnecessary curb on ideas.

It is very difficult the first time, and gets easier with each project, as experience makes you aware of the likely expenses. You cannot plan your budget, allot the hours it will take to complete a costume, or tick off on your list that you have finished a particular job, as you can for a scripted piece. You have to leave avenues open for director, writer and actors, and indeed yourself, if you are the designer, to have new ideas and be able to use them.

Try to keep at least a quarter of your budget, however small the total, in reserve for the technical and dress rehearsals – you are bound to need it, and if you do not, you can always use it for last-minute improvements to your work. You have to keep the seesaw balanced between invention and practicality, and judge

Different aspects of the production being discussed in rehearsal.
Photo: Hannah Bicât

DESIGNING AND MAKING COSTUMES

the moment when a definite decision has to be made, so that the costume will be ready for the actor to wear at the dress rehearsal. Arrange with the stage manager or production manager to get funds early if you are going to start work before the whole company assembles.

See Chapters 8 and 9 for more reflections on budgeting issues.

DESIGNING THE COSTUMES

Costumes for scripted theatre, and for devised or improvised work, make different demands on the designer. You may be used to working with a reliable cast list from a script you can study. It is easy to be irritated, or panic stricken, or both by the fact that you really do not know what will happen. It is difficult not to long for definite decisions. Keep cool, have patience and confidence. Remember that all the company's random ideas and decisions relating to costume will come to you to weave into your final designs. You must leave space, time and money for this to happen.

Very little is required to suggest a period and a character to an audience. In asking actors to participate in the design of their own costume, as you must do when the work is devised, you are opening the door to hundreds of disconnected ideas from different imaginations. An actress may have a mental picture of herself in full Victorian costume with wig, boots and accessories reproduced with historical accuracy, and the actor playing her husband may see himself in the breeches and boots of an earlier period, which he feels suit his role. Neither idea may coincide with the way the director, writer or designers sees the style of the play. Your job as a costume designer can be the gathering and refining of these random perspectives to create a cohesive picture for the audience.

When there is a clear story line and a definite cast list, you will design in a more conventional manner. Changes will still occur, new ideas and characterizations emerge, and your costumes and state of mind should stay open for these changes. However, you will know how many characters you have to dress. You can discuss and design the costumes in advance and work out how much it will cost in time and labour to produce them. The drawings will be ready to show the actors on the first day of rehearsal. The designs may be added to or altered, new ideas are bound to emerge in rehearsal, but as long as you have reserved a reasonable proportion of your budget (perhaps twenty-five per cent) you should be able to cope with these possibilities.

Often the information that would have enabled you to design before the start of rehearsals does not exist; the cast is large, and time and funds are limited. A basic costume for the players can be decided in advance and will serve as a background to the detailed accessories that will delineate each character. These can be designed as the actors' roles grow in rehearsal. In addition to the appearance of the basic costume you must consider:

- **The silhouette.** Should this echo the silhouette of the costume of the time, for example, a full, long skirt and a close-fitting top for a Victorian woman, or should the costume merely cover the body and make no particular statement? The basic costume must allow for any particular movement envisaged by the movement director or choreographer.
- **The colour.** A neutral colour, such as grey, beige, cream and, of course, white or black, lends itself best to adaptations. Sometimes, however, it can work to dress actors in the same shape and texture but in different colours. Colour should be decided upon in conjunction with the set designer, and it is most helpful if the lighting designer is present at this meeting.

113

Design showing the basic costume of a spotted dress and the additions of skirts, coats and accessories, which alter its function.

- **The texture.** A slightly rough textured cloth will be more adaptable in the light than a smooth textured one. You can make cheap calico, or even hessian, look rich and luscious in stage light, but cheap polyester lining material will look like polyester lining material in almost all circumstances. Jersey-type cloth is most useful as it hangs well, comes in many weights and finishes, and often does not need hemming.
- **The cost.** It is no good designing something wonderful if you cannot afford to show it to the audience.
- **The practicality.** How long it will take to cut, fit and make? Consider the skill of the people who are making the costumes and how long they have for the job. Design work will sink or swim by the accurate assessment of this apparently mundane consideration.

THE WORKROOM AND THE MAKING OF COSTUMES

The design and wardrobe department for a devised production must be approachable and available. This workroom can be organized, if not set up, before the start of rehearsals. You may, as designer, be making the costumes

Realistic Creativity

If a costume cannot be created with the human and technical resources available, scrap it and find a more practical idea. This can be miserably disappointing to the designer, worse for the maker and confidence-destroying for the actor, but the most wonderful ideas, the most successful costumes and the happiest of actors can emerge from this rigorous process.

yourself or you may have a wardrobe department making them for you: you will need to check table space, power points and light, so that you can rearrange anything inappropriate or bodge up a substitute.

Try to ascertain the measurements of actors before the start of the project, when time is short. The production manager will send out a measurement form or liase with actor's agents to obtain these. Or, in a small company, do it yourself. Measuring can eat up time during rehearsal, which could have been used more creatively. If you have measurements, it may be possible to make much of a basic costume before rehearsals start. Shoes can be bought so that they are ready to fit on the first day of rehearsal.

There is a particular value in devising actors wearing their costumes for rehearsal. Actors cease to feel dressed up and begin to live in their costumes. Everyone, including the director, movement director and lighting designer, become familiar with the way actors look and can judge when the basic costume needs additions for a particular role. Working in this way means that a fair proportion, perhaps half or three-quarters, of the money will have been spent before rehearsals start. The rest will be used to adapt the basic design during rehearsals.

REHEARSALS

Your work in rehearsal is to translate ideas into a universally understandable visual form. The best possible situation for a designer of devised theatre is to be in the rehearsal room all the time. Establish early on that your presence can be helpful and timesaving, as well as a creative boon for the director. It can work well to have a small table in the corner of the rehearsal room as your work station. The company will come and discuss ideas as they occur and you can try them out together. This can save hours and days of working on misunderstandings that may not be used in performance. You must work subtly and quietly so as not to disturb rehearsals, and listen and draw more than you talk.

The next best thing is to be able to hear from the workroom what is going on on-stage. Explain to the director and stage manager that you would like to be called from the workroom to rehearsal if a costume is being discussed, so that you can be present to listen and give informed and practical help.

Get to know the actors and make sure they can talk to you easily without a complicated system of appointments. The more you watch and listen, the more you are likely to keep abreast of the ideas and emotions of the company, and be able to reflect them in your designs. Excellent communication with the stage management is essential. Actors delight in being given a chance to develop their character out of a costume and vice versa (see Chapter 3 for more details). Ask them for notes of any costume-related events or ideas that occur in the course of the day's work. Produce drawings or concrete ideas quickly to discuss with director and actors. It is difficult for them to imagine the whole picture the audience will see on-stage. Their costume ideas will be more appropriate if that picture is made clear to them; it will help if actors can see an example or drawing of the basic costume they will be wearing, even if it changes later.

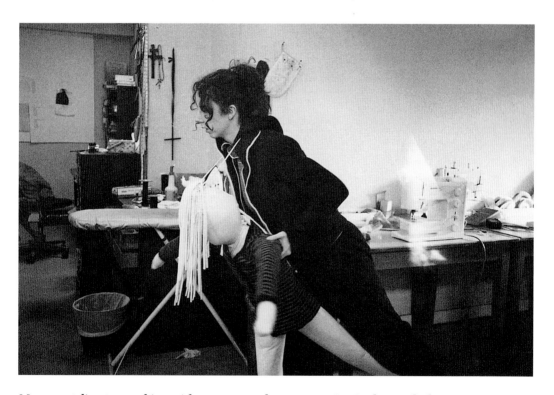

Movement director working with a puppet under construction in the wardrobe.
Photo: Tina Bicât

Actors experimenting with a giant's hand in rehearsal. Photo: Hannah Bicât

Actors, as well as armies, march on their feet. Shoes are expensive, and must fit and feel right to the actors, as well as look right for the characters who wear them. The slow wearing in of shoes will avoid blisters and discomfort. Decide on footwear early and implement the decision, so that the correct shoes can be worn in rehearsal.

PLAYING WITH COSTUMES IN REHEARSAL

It can be difficult to demonstrate to young actors and students of costume design how very little is required to suggest a period and a character to an audience. It is easier for all actors to have some physical realization of a costume idea to play with.

Providing Visual Images for the Company

Actors who have seen their costumes early on will be more likely to have ideas in rehearsal that will be practical and will marry with the overall design concept. Show them rough sketches, photocopies or roughly made mock-ups of costume additions. Have a full-length mirror available. Make sure fittings are unhurried and allow time for experiment with movement. Leave plenty of time to create these new ideas: they will keep coming until the dress rehearsal.

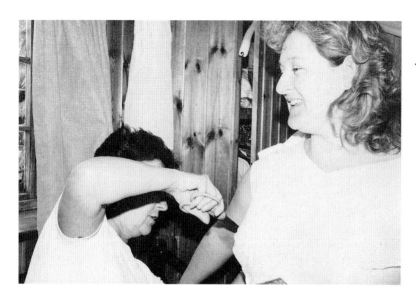

Actor and maker work together at a fitting.

They can easily imagine a piece of rag is a delicate lace shawl or a length of old broomstick is an eighteenth-century silver-topped walking cane. When the accessories for a costume are not designed in advance and the inspiration for them is taken directly from the actors' work, it is essential to have these representational bits and pieces of costume to hand.

Example

The barefoot actor dressed in his basic costume of loose cream calico trousers and tunic is playing a slave-driver in seventeenth-century Spain. He needs some simple, significant garment that will transform him, speedily and simply, from a nice young man to a sinister, squalid and lecherous object of terror. During the rehearsal he begins to speak with his chin pressed sideways to his chest and his back hunched. The director wants more – more sinister, more squalid, more lecherous. The actor is handed one shoe, one of his own shoes, not a period shoe. The moment he begins to work in the single shoe he starts to drag the shod foot behind him and approach people crab-wise. He is passed a single black trouser leg (it has been hastily chopped off an old pair of tights and a strap of elastic and safety pins braces it over one shoulder) and helped to put it on. The feeling of that unequal, awkward garment adds security to his growing characterization, and invention to his improvisation. Had it not, had he felt uneasy with the feeling the clothes gave him, then the idea could have been chucked away. A few words and the mock-up of the costume explained an idea clearly and quickly, with no time and money wasted.

After rehearsal the idea was discussed in more detail and the trouser leg, its brace and the shoe were designed and made. The shape suggested a codpiece at the crutch and made the actor's legs appear to be different lengths. The boot added a period detail. Meanwhile the actor used the mock-up in rehearsal.

THE TECHNICAL AND DRESS REHEARSALS

Running the costume department during the technical rehearsal of devised theatre requires

Using a piece of cloth in rehearsal to represent a more complicated headress. Photo: Tina Bicât

The Slave Driver

A basic thick cotton costume is worn by all men.

Black lycra trouser leg with basic costume bunching out of it.

bare feet.

Design. Final design for slave driver showing how the rehearsal trouser leg became a costume.
Photo: Tina Bicât

Actors and designer deciding on a make-up style for the production. Photo: Tina Bicât

special skills. All through rehearsals you have been encouraging change and invention. Now, with tact and firmness, you must make sure everyone realizes that the time for new ideas has passed. You must be in the position of being sure that all costumes are complete, fit, work in the quick changes and look right in the lights on-stage. You cannot do this if new ideas are still emerging. There will be emergencies when things do not work and changes and alterations are essential, but the design has to be set at this point. And, at last, you know how much of your budget you have left to improve costumes if you want to. This is the time for the final list of jobs the workroom must complete before the dress rehearsal.

By the morning of the dress rehearsal, the costumes should be finished in every detail. The picture that you have been building in your head, in cloth and on paper can be seen by the whole company in the habitat created by the set and lighting designers. The complete picture that the audience will see with you, on the first night.

EXERCISES

Exercise 1: Playing with Costume in Mind or Mirror

This is for design students, to suggest period costume or character with simple signs.

Imagine a man in a black high-necked jersey, black trousers and black footwear:

- give him some Brylcreem for his hair, a cigarette and a bootlace tie that shows up against his black jersey and narrow his trousers, and he becomes a 1960s Teddy boy;
- give him a top hat and a walking stick: he becomes a gentleman from the past and from the higher strata of society;
- give him a battered top hat, roll up his trouser legs and take away his stick and his

Checklist for Design and Wardrobe

This is an example of a check list for a devised project. It gives some guidelines and suggests questions that need to be answered. It would of course be different for every project.

Research:
- Study the source material.
- Who was wearing what at the time?
- What was happening historically and socially?
- How did the people live their daily lives?

Pre-production:
- What is the style, genre, feeling of the production?
- Will actors play many roles or just one each?
- How many actors?
- What are their measurements and shoe sizes?

Budget:
- How much is the costume budget?
- How do you obtain it or reclaim it, and from whom?
- Will the company pay for the actors to have fittings before rehearsals start, or do you have to rely on goodwill?
- Is there money available for you to shop before the rehearsals start?
- Does the company have any special deals or accounts with suppliers?
- Can you offer programme credits or free tickets in exchange for goods or help?

Workroom:
- Organize a space as close to the rehearsal room as possible.
- Check power-points, lighting, tables and equipment.
- Try to give all workers a small area of private territory.

Altering the shape of a costume in rehearsal. Photo: Hannah Bicât

shoes: you have left him in the same era but taken away his status;
- give him back the stick, some boots, a belt, a forage cap and a military attitude: he is a soldier.

Imagine a woman in a close-fitting black top and opaque black tights and shoes:

- give her a long skirt and a black neckband and put her hair up: she goes back in time 100 years or so;

- take off the neckband, hitch the skirt upon either hip and let some of her hair down: she goes back another couple of hundred years;
- take away the shoes and wind a cloth round head and shoulders: she goes back even further in time.

With these examples as a starting point, use things that lie around the rehearsal room, such as pencils (cigarettes and feathers), umbrellas (sticks and weapons or parasols), coats, bags, sweaters and hats, to add further information about a character. The object is to clarify rather than complicate the picture. An actor could suck a pencil and look like a murdering savage with a blow pipe, a child with a lollipop or a vamp with a cigarette. Why? What makes the audience imagine one or the other? What could the designer give the actor to help show the right information? The effects should be tested on the other members of the group to see if they clarify or confuse the message in the costume.

Exercise 2: Transforming Objects

For actors, to demonstrate how objects and clothes can be given new life in the devising rehearsal room.

Ask the actors to stand in a large circle. Give one of them an umbrella and tell them they are a mother and the umbrella is a baby. Ask the actor to carry the baby across the circle and give it to someone else with a suggestion for a change of character, i.e. this is my baby and I am giving it to a fisherman.

The new possessor of the umbrella re-invents the umbrella as perhaps a fishing rod or a boat, and carries it to yet another actor with the information: this is my fishing rod, boat or whatever, and I am giving it to Queen Victoria. And so the game proceeds.

A big apron, a pair of large floppy pyjama or track-suit trousers and a pair of tights are all excellent and adaptable articles for this game and can be imagined as animals, belts, hangman's nooses, hats and hair, and endless other costumes and props.

8 STAGE MANAGEMENT
Alison King

The stage manager responsible for the technical management of a scripted show has a script to study and a model box, which gives an impression of the set and sketches of the costumes before starting the practical process of creating the show. Devised theatre has none of these starting blocks and this can be extremely disconcerting for stage management. It is like venturing on a walking holiday with no boots, tent or maps!

The stage management department is responsible for organizing the practical side of the show and co-ordinating it from the first discussions to its opening night and beyond. This will include co-ordinating the production team and the stage crew from the rehearsal period through to the fit-up of the set, the running of the show's scene and costume changes, and the cueing of the lights and sound. In other words, the stage management department is responsible for the hands-on side of everything!

Production managers take responsibility for running the stage management crew and organizing the creative team. They control the budget and oversee all the practical aspects of the show from the set building and the venue to health and safety.

Deputy stage managers are based in rehearsals as a communication point between the director and the rest of the team. They work closely with the actors, recording the moves (blocking) and will eventually cue/operate the show when it moves onto the stage. They create the prompt copy, the bible of a show, which contains all the information needed to run the show. The prompt copy will contain the script cue sheets with the actors' moves recorded, all the lighting and sound cues written in, and a list of where all the props and set go. The prompt copy should be easy to read and understand, so that in an emergency anyone can work from it.

Assistant stage managers help organize props for the show and act as crew and runners.

However, do not be alarmed if you find you are a one-man band! These roles are often condensed for a small-scale theatre or low-budget show. You can cover all roles if you work closely with the company and maintain a realistic and honest approach about how much you can achieve. It is important to be clear about this when you are taking the job or talking to the director or producer. You can often delegate part of your work or get help from a loyal band of volunteers.

The stage management crew is the backbone of the show and its creative process. They help realize the dreams and ideas of the creative team from a practical point of view and are responsible for structuring the workloads, as well as working hands-on. In devised theatre, this process can be slow to start and it can be hard for stage management to get their teeth into the work and feel part of the team. This chapter aims to provide confidence and encourage the natural

Post show clear-up – a stage manager's task.

resourcefulness and initiative of the person in charge of stage management.

Devised theatre can liberate the creative team and its actors. For stage management it can be the greatest challenge of your career and you will need, above all else, patience and a sense of humour.

PREPARATION AND RESEARCH

If the work is based on a novel or a story, read it several times before the first meeting, and if the piece is historical, research the period.

Then you can use the meeting to obtain as much information as possible with which to start work, and show the team that you are enthusiastic, keen and already have some interesting and pertinent thoughts. There is nothing worse than stage management who have not read the script before the first meeting or appear uninformed about the show's subject. It is part of their role to be knowledgeable. And it is a great chance, if you have not worked with the team before, to start building a relationship. Early trust built amongst the creative team and stage management is vital for a successful show.

PRE-PRODUCTION DISCUSSIONS AND MEETINGS

Every member of the creative team will want to meet and exchange ideas – be on time for these meetings or, preferably, early, and pack a diary, notebook and pens. It is vital that the stage management have a first meeting with the producer, director and writer, and gauge the time frame and the budget. Find out what they expect of you, so that your role is clearly defined. Gather as much information as possible about the projected style of the show.

The director and the producer are the most important people to stage management. You need to climb into their minds and study them closely so you can learn to pre-empt their thoughts or, at the very least, understand where they are coming from. Later on in the creative process they can become your greatest ally or worst enemy; you need to be their support. Often the stage manager will be the director's and producer's voice, and represent them to the rest of the team. The producer especially will want to hand over the practicalities of the show to the production management team, so that they can observe rehearsals and be a sounding board for the

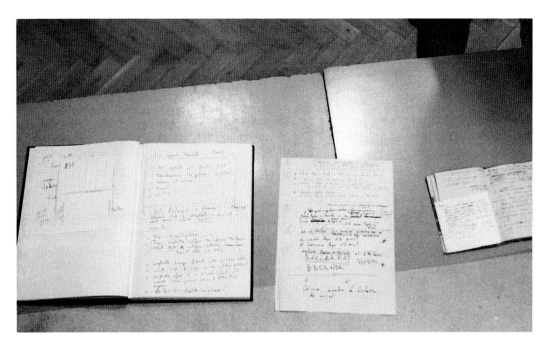

A devising prompt book must be developed during rehearsals.

director. An experienced stage manager can speak on behalf of the director and producer and be right. After the first meeting you should have a clear idea of how the company wishes to work.

If you have been asked to organize the next, more general, meeting, which will include the set, costume and lighting designers, set up the room with a large table, plenty of chairs and possibly refreshments. Before the meeting make sure a contact sheet with everyone's phone numbers is available to keep those lines of communication open.

The stage manager is often asked to run production meetings. It is important that they run them, and do not take over. They need to make sure that every area of the production team gets to talk and that ideas can flow freely from department to department. As the project will still be a mass of ideas, it is important that you nurture the ideas and allow the creativity to flow. Be a *yes* person and not a *no* person (or at least a 'good suggestion, we'll explore that later' person). Agree that most things can be accomplished and try to suggest ways that ideas can be realized. At this stage it is important not to get bogged down with systems and rules, though a voice of reason will not go amiss.

Prompt Point

The stage manager is a crucial communicator. But what is going on in the head of the director and producer? See Chapters 1 and 9 for some suggestions!

When devising theatre, all the boundaries need to be explored. Belief in the project is paramount. For as many ideas that get dismissed as ludicrous, as many will be brilliant pieces of creative genius. The role of the stage manager at these meetings is to support, observe, encourage and listen to everyone, record everything and then act accordingly, wielding notebook. You will also need to apply instinct on which ideas are the 'ones' but that comes later. In devised theatre, time and imaginations often run out, or wild, or both, because so much is being created during the process. There will be different questions for each department.

Before the meeting draws to a close:

- Make sure that each department is happy and feels that they have covered enough ground.
- Help organize individual meetings between different team members
- Make everyone agree to achievable goals within a definite time frame.

- Decide the next meeting date for the whole team.
- Make sure that the budget has been discussed and allocated accordingly; if the time-scale and money are short the creative team will want to get going.
- Make sure that the list for the stage management team is in hand and that there is a reasonable amount of work to be getting on with. The work may be still at the ideas stage and there may not be anything tangible to work with yet, but it is your job to squeeze out the ideas and find yourself tasks to do. They are there if you look closely enough. You may have time to research the subject matter more thoroughly or explore and familiarize yourself with the venues for the performance.

THE BUDGET

The producer may allocate the money to the different practical departments, or pass on the

---

Checklists of Some Points to Ascertain from the Creative Team at First Meetings

NB If the team has worked together before, then some of these will be irrelevant.

Director:
- style
- budget
- where idea has come from
- working methods
- expectations of stage manager.

Producer:
- venue
- time frame
- salary

- expectations of stage manager.
- company history

Costume/set designer:
- extra team members needed
- work-place/room/shop
- method of working
- budget expectations.

Any known hirers/unusual finds

Lighting/sound designer:
- extra team members
- any known technical requirements
- method of working
- budget expectations.

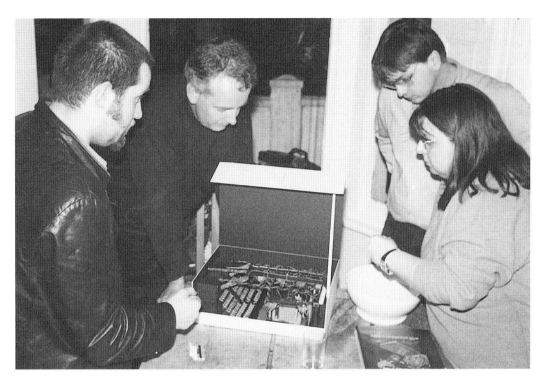

Production meeting in progress. *Photo: Tina Bicât*

total sum to the production manager to distribute accordingly. Often co-ordinating and running a budget is the job of the production manager. A good head for numbers is essential, as well as a practical and slightly pessimistic view of how much things cost. That way the projected budget will be generous and you can cut from it – and you will need to. Every member of the creative team will want, and will tell you that they need, the most money; you need to listen but trust your instincts. To understand the implications of budgets see Chapter 9.

Allocating the budget for devised theatre is extremely hard, as at the early stage there may be no idea where the piece is going or how it will grow. It is important that, as the stage manager, you remain flexible and open to ideas

and do not refuse everything on the grounds of lack of money. The secret is to try to ascertain early where the scales will tip. Here are some examples of the sort of questions to ask yourself in order to help divide your budget:

- If the piece of theatre being created is a period piece, will costumes cost more?
- If it's outdoors, what are you using for the set and will lighting requirements increase?
- If the piece is to be in a proscenium arch theatre with a fly tower, is there going to be flying, of any scenery or cloths?
- Does the set designer envisage scene changes, for example, from outdoors to indoors?
- How many characters are there (this may be a rough estimate)?

Two Crucial Budgeting Tips

Keep a contingency fund to be given to the most desperate department later in the process and always tell each department that they have ten per cent less than you have allotted: this allows for an overspend and for any unforeseen circumstances and last-minute additions, inevitable with devised theatre.

Stage manager making something out of nothing – needs must. Photo: Tina Bicât

There will be times nearing the end or in production week when there really is no more time and money and, however good the brain wave, you have to say no. If a member of the creative team has an amazing but expensive idea, then beg, borrow and steal (out of skips, etc!) to make it a possible reality. Stage management needs great charm and powers of persuasion. They need to be able to sweet talk everyone, spot a bargain, charm a trader out of a deal and act like a hard-nosed negotiator. This is the only way small budgets and theatre can operate.

Reward friends, relatives and businesses with a thank you in a programme, free tickets or even an advert or special billing. If you are

Budget Checklist

Headings, questions and areas of consideration:

- set: fee, paint and materials for set builder;
- props: hiring/making/buying/running props/fees for prop makers;
- costume/wigs: allocated budget plus making and purchasing costs (e.g. shoes), assistant fees/work room costs;
- lighting: gel, hiring, special effects, assistant fees;
- sound: recording costs, e.g. studio/PA system, outside musicians, microphones, instrument hire.
- fit-up labour: how many extra people are needed during the get in-daily rate/expenses
- transport: how is the set getting to the theatre and how many trips will be required? – remember the get out;
- miscellaneous: for the unforeseen;
- contingency: ten per cent of your production budget for safe-keeping.

lent something of value, insure it and take responsibility for its safe-keeping. There is nothing worse than abusing someone's generosity and returning the item spoiled.

You can make an item, weighing up the cost against the time in manpower and the finished look. Or scavenge in your mum's garage, a skip, charity shop, workshop or obscure shops and house clearance places. Expect to go anywhere and everywhere. It is like being an archaeologist digging for hidden treasure.

REHEARSALS

The devising theatre company is poised and ready to start. Like the start-up line for the 100 metres, the gun is about to go off!

Even though you will be as far ahead as possible with the preparation, there will be a lot to achieve now the show is being created. The first few days may find you hanging around as ideas get tested, tried and thrown out. Do not panic – just observe quietly and calmly, and make sure that there is a member of the stage management team in rehearsals all or least 95 per cent of the time. The creative team are then able to shout out their ideas and requests, and these can be filtered quickly to the relevant person and be processed quickly.

One of the most important stage management jobs is communication. Tell everyone everything, no matter how trivial it

Rehearsal in progress. Photo: Tina Bicât

Prompt Point

A number of chapters discuss the way chance ideas or discoveries can be of critical importance: see Chapters 5 and 7. But such discoveries do have consequences for everyone – including the stage management team.

---

appears. You are the most qualified messenger in the whole process – deliver. Always write everything down; do not trust your memory. From here on in you will be working long hours against the clock and will be exhausted.

At the end of each day's rehearsal develop a routine of grabbing the director for a quick chat. Most directors will resist this, but insist. Check how the day went, show them your continuing support and enthusiasm for the project, and have ready your list of points to clarify. You will find the director will suddenly have practical thoughts and ask you about that mad elusive idea they were trying earlier. For example, you might ask, 'That white sheet that you were using for a warm up game, are you really going to use it to represent mountains?'; 'Yes' replies the director, 'and, wait, what are the chances of projecting onto it?'; quick – grab the set and costume designers to join the chat.

It is also important that you keep checking how the creative departments are getting on. How are they doing with their spending and are they are feeling happy and confident? Spend a few moments sitting with them, getting to know them and absorbing how much they still have to do. You must retain an overview of each department. However behind you get, and however desperate the process may become, do not become unhinged and lose your cool. Always appear confident and in control. If necessary, leave the room to break down! Everyone will look to you for support

and encouragement, and you must be prepared and able to give it. In devised theatre there really will be desperate times because the process is being created around you. There is no rulebook to follow, so remember that and keep smiling.

During the rehearsal process you will be rushing around getting the stuff needed in rehearsals, beginning to assemble the props, organizing set-building materials. Lighting and sound considerations will also become paramount as time progresses and you will have to make sure that props are tried out and used in rehearsals. Liaison with the venue regarding technical matters, get-in times and such-like will need to be planned. You need to keep all the departments communicating, to look after the actors and to lend your support

Rehearsals and experiments. Photo: Tina Bicât

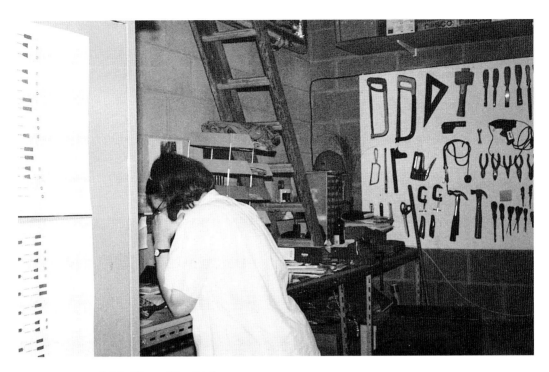

Stage manager's kit. Photo: Tina Bicât

to the director and producer. Clearly this is only an overview of your involvement in the rehearsal process but you can get an idea of how busy you will be.

It is vital that you are organized and keep lists of things to do, which will need updating everyday. For example, if the director needs a rehearsal prop, get that first, before a lighting effect of less immediate importance. Try to arrange production meetings with the whole team at the end of each week so they can update and discuss ideas and problems. These meetings are more vital in devised theatre, in order to make the growing process apparent to everyone.

During rehearsals you are the lynch pin, you need to hold everyone together and drive the process forward. In devising theatre, glitches will be hit and creativity will stop. Help by calming nerves or advising everyone to sleep on it. Your response at all times needs to be quick, as time is precious. Also, as busy as you will be, you will have a broader view than the rest of the creative team because you are slightly removed creatively. This can be invaluable, as you can think what you would feel as an audience member viewing the whole product. Offer your opinion, if asked, or if you know the particular team member very well and there is a lot of mutual trust and respect. Remember that sensitivity is needed.

There will come a time when you will need to get tough and say no; this can be hard, but necessary. Projects can fall apart if creative people lose track of time and practicalities, and it will be up to you to rein them back without compromising the artistry too much. One way of dealing with this is to set deadlines by drawing up a schedule of the developing process with the director.

Agree a cut-off point that will allow enough time to make, find or build all that will be required. Use the heads of the departments to set the points with yourself and the director. For example, if the rehearsal process is four weeks, agree that after two weeks you can have a clear idea of what props, sets and costumes are needed, and a definite cut-off point at the end of the penultimate week. Encourage the director to stagger through a run of the piece by the end of the second week, and get key company members to attend. You can be flexible but realistic goals should help keep the project on track.

PRODUCTION WEEK

Production week is when the piece of theatre that has been created starts to come to life on stage, the final touches are put to it and the last jigsaw piece is placed. It is your week and ultimately what you have been hired for. It is a truly mad week and with all the planning in

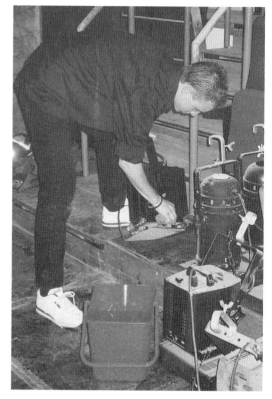

Preparing lights prior to rigging.

Checklist

Stage manager's equipment for rehearsals includes:

- notebook/pencils/pen/rubber/hole punch/stapler;
- scissors/screwdrivers/hammer/adjustable spanner/drill;
- tape-measure;
- insulation tape/gaffa tape/Sellotape;
- stop-watch for timing;
- show contact list containing everyone's number;

- A to Z, map of the area plus Yellow Pages;
- petty cash for travel, tea, coffee, etc.;
- rehearsal provisions, e.g. tea, coffee, cups, etc.;
- rehearsal props;
- kit for actors to play with (based on type of show), e.g. sticks/card/elastic/coloured pens, etc.

It is all a headache – production week.

the world there will still be surprises, problems and stress. One of the secrets of its success lies in a good production schedule.

The production week normally starts the weekend before the show opens. That first weekend you and your team will get in and assemble the set in the theatre space. Once that is done the designer and team will move in for any painting that has not happened off site, maybe a back wall or a floor. Always schedule floor painting for the end of a day.

Once the set is up, the lighting designer and team will focus the lights, which they may have rigged either before the set went in or around the set: you will decide. You, as stage manager, need to assist with the set and the lights, check their positions and safety, and have the final say on their practical placing and fit up. When the lighting team are

focusing, you need to be on hand to clarify actors' positions, as you will know the show better than anyone else on the team. You are the voice of the director and the producer during this week and what you say goes – it has to if the show is going to open on time. This is the week that the show begins to get handed over to you.

During this week you have to learn the technical workings of the show and, if you are operating or cueing the show, where the lighting and sound cues go. With devised theatre there may still not be a script, just notes, so instead of a prompt copy, you may have just cue sheets. Use the plotting session of the lights and the technical rehearsal to make sure the show is well-documented and easy for someone else to read, just in case you go under a bus.

The Production Schedule

We will presume that you are getting into a theatre and are fitting up on the Friday and opening on the following Friday. This is a typical production schedule and will show you how to include and make time.

Friday 23rd July

10.30am–6.30pm	Rehearsals as normal in rehearsal room.
10.00am–1.00pm, 2.00pm–6.00pm	Lights to be rigged on stage.
1.00pm–2.00pm	Lunch.
10.00am–6.00pm	Work on set in theatre, base coat on floor.

Saturday 24th July

10.30am–1.00pm	Lighting team in theatre finish rig/focus.
10.30am–6.30pm	Production team rigging set.
1.00pm–2.00pm	Lunch.
12.30pm–7.00pm	Cast rehearse in rehearsal room (two runs through).

Sunday 25th July

	Cast day off
12.00pm till finish	Production team assemble in theatre, fit up set, paint floor and varnish last thing.
1.00pm–2.00pm	Lunch.

(NB: The set has had three days to fit up but you could work later nights if you did not have all this time).

Monday 26th July

10.30am	Cast called to rehearsal.
10.30am–all day	Technical work in theatre, focus/pre-plot, etc. plus set work, i.e. painting, as required.
1.00pm–2.00pm	Lunch.

Tuesday 27th July

	Production team continue. Work as necessary.
10.30am–6.30pm	Rehearsal in theatre all day.

(NB: It is a good idea to familiarize cast with space, but this is time for you if you have over run!)

1.30pm–2.30pm	Lunch.
7.00pm–10.00pm	Plot lights in theatre (technical call) director/producer/LX designer/stage manager/costume designer called

Wednesday 28th July

10.00am	Cast called.
10.15am–12.00 noon	Costume call.
12.30pm–1.30pm	Technical rehearsal.

1.30pm–2.30pm	Lunch.
2.30pm–6.00pm	Technical rehearsal continues.
6.00pm–7.00pm	Dinner break.
7.00pm–10.00pm	Technical rehearsal continues.
10.00pm	Finish.

Thursday 29th July

10.00am–12.30pm	Work in theatre as required/ finish technical rehearsal.
12.30pm	Cast called.
1.25pm	Half- hour call.
2.00pm	Dress rehearsal 1.
4.15pm	Dress rehearsal finish.
4.30pm–5.30pm	Work as required.
5.30pm–7.00pm	Break.
6.25pm	Half hour call.
7.00pm	Dress rehearsal 2.
9.15pm	Finish dress.
9.45pm	Rehearsals finish.

Friday 30th July

10.00am–12.30pm	Work in theatre as required.
12.30pm	Cast called.
1.25pm	Half hour call.
2.00pm	Dress rehearsal 3
4.15pm	Dress finish.
4.30pm -5.30pm	Work as required
5.30pm–7.00pm	Break
6.25pm	½-hour call
7.00pm	1st Show!
9.30pm	Finish

Please note that this production schedule is subject to change. The cast and crew will be given suitable notice.

Thank you in anticipation for your patience and co-operation.

The only way to get through a production week is to clear your diary of all other engagements and give yourself wholly to the show. Everyone is pushed to their limits and will work long hours and often late into the night. Offer encouragement, stay calm and as relaxed as is humanly possible. It cannot be stressed enough how vital it is to keep it together. Small gestures of making tea or a drink or those all-important late night 'chips and chocolate runs' show the team that you care.

A technical rehearsal – notes and all. Photo: Tina Bicât

As production manager you will have prepared and circulated a production schedule by working out how much time is needed by each department and allocating it accordingly. Stick it everywhere – in the dressing rooms, crew room, work rooms and theatre space, so that it is a constant reminder to everyone. Try to stick to it as much as possible, but be prepared to turn back, rewrite and radically alter it as you go along – it is there as a guide. You will need to hide time so that as things start to run behind schedule you can release it for the experiments that will still be happening with the set, costume, lights and so on. The show has to open, but if it can open with breathing space and everyone having had some sleep, then so much the better. It is part of your job to try and achieve this.

THE TECHNICAL REHEARSAL

The technical rehearsal is run by the production manager or stage manager and is for the stage management and the technical team. It is not a rehearsal for actors, but rather a rehearsal for set, costume, sound and lights, though of course the actors are there. The set, costumes, lighting and sound come together and stage management have to co-ordinate it all. It is important that you go over things again and again and again, if you or any of your crew feel it is necessary. That is what the rehearsal is there for. Keep calm. If anyone gets annoyed or impatient at the repetition they are wrong to do so. Do not feel pressurized to move on if you are not happy. If you are the stage manager, then you and only you communicate with everyone and field messages. The communication goes through a chain. All messages should be communicated through the stage manager. This will keep it running smoothly and not have everyone shouting at once. If the operators are in a technical box miles away, set up some cans (communication headsets) to keep lines of communication open and place yourself in the auditorium or at the prompt desk in the wings. You have to be strong, clear and concise. See Chapter 1 on handing over rehearsals to the technical team

Explain to the company how the technical rehearsal is going to work. This is a useful speech, as it shows the power shift from the director and producer to the stage manager. In script-based productions, the minimum rehearsal time will be at least three times the length of the play but often much longer. In devised theatre, the technical rehearsal will be particularly long because the process will still be happening and information will not be as prepared. Relax, accept this and do not worry. Talk to the creative team and find out their needs. It may be useful to have a costume call, or to work all the scene changes; this can reduce technical time by preparing the actors.

THE DRESS REHEARSAL

This follows the technical rehearsal and, unless someone dies, you never stop. Try to fit two dress rehearsals into the production schedule, so that if time runs out you can lose one and free up time. Notes will be given afterwards, mainly by the director and the producer. Listen carefully, do not get defensive or blame anyone else, clarify points if necessary write the note down and amend the error.

Once you have got through this and approach your opening show, relax, enjoy it and let the audience's response show you what all the stress and hard work has achieved. You may have vowed, 'That's it, never again!' but when you hear the applause and see the show that you have helped pull together, you will want to do it all over again.

9 PRODUCTION
Charlotte Cunningham

Producing a devised piece of theatre is probably the most creative way to be a producer in the field of live performance. Whereas film producers are allowed to make all of the decisions about their chosen project and interfere at any stage in the production, theatre producers often get left sorting out the management and finances, and only step in when the director cannot cope any more. However, when it comes to devised theatre, the producer needs to be completely involved and utterly dedicated to ensure that the project comes to fruition.

The idea behind a devised piece of theatre could come from many different sources. As the producer, you could pick up a book one day and decide that the story in that book must be put on stage; a director could come and talk to you about a period in history that has inspired him to create a piece of theatre; an organization could approach you and suggest a theme that is relevant to them (e.g. genetics or drug abuse); a favourite actor could decide that they would like to create a certain character for the stage in a framework that does not exist yet; or a costume designer could convince you to devise a new theatrical odyssey for children.

Whatever the genesis of the project, you as the producer must be utterly convinced that there is something in the idea that will appeal to other people. Once you are committed to the project you will have to persuade an entire theatrical team, funders or backers, venues, marketing and press people, and the target audience, that this is a worthwhile endeavour. Assuming that you still have no cast or creative team, and obviously no script, the main asset you have now is your own enthusiasm and conviction about the project. In the initial stages of the project you are its ambassador, while in the latter stages you become its diplomat. The first rule about producing this kind of work is therefore to follow your gut instincts and only do it if you really believe in it!

CONCEPTION AND PLANNING

As soon as you have decided that the project you are about to embark on is the right one and that nothing like it has been seen in your town or city for decades, you start to think about the practicalities.

- What type of people do you need to make it work?
- How many people do you need ?

Prompt Point

How do you test whether a good story or idea is a good theatrical one? See Chapters 1 and 4.

- When are you planning on doing this?
- Should you be looking for a theatre space or a disused power station as a venue?
- What audience will it appeal to? Is there potential for education work in the story?
- How much will it cost?
- Who may be interested in giving some money towards this project and why?

There are quite a few chicken and egg situations involved in this kind of planning, and ideally you have to tackle the questions one by one, starting at the top, to make it work. If you fail to do this, you can get stuck very quickly: For instance, you think of a perfect sponsor – an organic supermarket chain for a project about Native American Indian healers. A large cast including Native American Indian shamans and drummers may appeal to them. But if you want to put it on in a disused power station, they might object. If you have not decided what audience it is for, then they cannot tell whether any of them are potential customers. And without some idea of cost, you do not know what to ask for! Back to square one.

What Type of People Do You Need?

If there is not already one on board, then obviously you need a director who is as passionate as you about the project – but the director must also be experienced in devising theatre. If the two of you then represent the core of the project, you need to decide who else you would like to be involved. Does the piece need original music and therefore a composer? Do you want to work with a writer during rehearsals or will it be a *dramaturg* (a continental title for someone who pulls together scripts but is not a writer)? Does the director want a choreographer to help with movement work? Who would be right to work on set and costume in this situation – do you need both? What level-headed production manager will agree to come on board and help make the project happen?

How Many People Do You Need?

At this stage it is better to plan for the ideal situation rather than the most practical – there will be time for that later. If you feel that the play would be best served by involving six actors and three musicians, then imagine that this is what you will have. You also need a creative team – again, plan for more rather than less: if someone comes along who combines costume, set and lighting talents then great, but expect initially to have all three. Devised theatre usually needs many hands towards the end of the rehearsal process and the beginning of performances – expect to recruit a small army of technicians and helpers in that last week of rehearsals.

When you are thinking about the last two areas – who and how many – you, as the producer. must take a step back from the artistic process and consider which of these people would interest both backers and audiences. If this is an entirely new piece, then the general public, including press, will need a hook to persuade them that it is going to be interesting. Maybe the composer has an incredible track record for composing film scores and has recently won an Oscar! Maybe you can persuade the team to cast an actor or actress whose name would give kudos to the production. Or is there enough of a hook in the source of the story to entice people in? It sounds depressing and lacking in artistic integrity to have to think about such things for this kind of a project, but without considering these points, the production might never happen.

When Are You Planning On Doing This?

It is important to set a time for when you think this project might happen. Obviously it might

139

Choosing the venue has major artistic and financial implications.
Photo: Hannah Bicât

change, but agreeing a date gives you a framework within which to think when you are talking to people. Furthermore, it may also have an impact on the type of venue. For example, December is not a good time for outdoor promenade shows in most of Western Europe.

What Kind of Venue Are You Looking For and What Audience Is Your Project Aimed At?

These two questions need more research to answer. The kind of venue that the piece will end up in depends on the creative team's artistic decisions and on the artistic decisions of the venue that will stage it. If the venue is a hired space, then this becomes more of a budget issue, but if not, then this is the time to start looking into places and organizing meetings to go and talk to the programmers. See also Chapter 2 for more ideas about venues.

At this point it is helpful to have something written down about the idea – ideally with some strong visual images and in some kind of pack. Programmers are very swayed by an image and if there is something really dynamic on the cover of what you send them, they are more likely to read further. A meeting with a venue programmer is preferable to just sending out information. You will be much more able to sell this idea to them face to face as you will be able to communicate your passion about it. If a meeting is impossible, then at least try to have a telephone conversation to communicate your excitement and pre-empt the information that you are going to send them.

The choice of venue will also have an impact on the audience that you will be targeting. Is the geographical location such that it will attract a young hip crowd or is it a perfect family location, e.g. a park or a museum? Does the venue already have a strong education policy that will help you target school audiences? You will also have to decide whether you want the content of the piece to be suitable for families with children or whether you want to explore issues that are simply not appropriate for this kind of audience. Do you want to ensure that people with disabilities can see this production? Is the space you have chosen accessible to this particular audience? Do you need the press to come to this performance to establish your company and make it easier to find funding the next time around, or is it more important to you to target a very local audience that may have a connection to your story or theme?

One of the ways to facilitate making these decisions, and even to start gathering a team, is to run one or more workshops based around your project during your conception stage. It may seem like extra organization, but the amount of information it will supply you with as the producer is invaluable.

How Much Will It Cost?

With some of fundamental decisions made about the show's content, venues and target audience, you can now start building a budget.

At this point your projected expenditure should look alarmingly large. Your challenge now is to find real ways of cutting it down and to find the corresponding income column – either through box office or through funding. There are many real ways of cutting down expenditure without compromising the artistic considerations. With enough time and energy, you should be able to borrow as many items of set and props and lighting equipment as possible.

Again, it is about contacting the companies that you need these things from ahead of time and convincing them that they want to help to make this project happen. You can cut down on people but, ideally, you may be able to discuss money issues with the team and get them all to agree to be paid a little less, rather than cutting an integral member. You should get some income from your box office, but this is not going to help your cash-flow during the production weeks and it cannot be depended on. If, for example, you are doing an outdoor show and it rains every day and you have to return the ticket money to the audience, then it is gone.

For this, as for most other projects, you will probably have to raise as large a sum as possible from funders and donors who will (hopefully) give their money ahead of the start date of the project. But remember that such organizations, whether spending public or private funds, will want to have some kind of stake in what you are doing.

Who May Be Interested In Giving Some Money Towards This Project and Why?

The first port of call for a project that is fairly experimental in its nature is probably your

Project Title	Production	Administration	Running	Touring
Fees	£	£	£	£
Director	£	£	£	£
Writer/dramaturg	£	£	£	£
Choreographer	£	£	£	£
Set designer	£	£	£	£
Costume designer	£	£	£	£
Lighting designer	£	£	£	£
Sound design	£	£	£	£
Production office	£	£	£	£
Production manager	£	£	£	£
Total Fees	£	£	£	£
Production	£	£	£	£
Set	£	£	£	£
Props	£	£	£	£
Costumes/wigs	£	£	£	£
Electrics	£	£	£	£
Sound	£	£	£	£
Transport	£	£	£	£
Miscellaneous	£	£	£	£
Fit up labour	£	£	£	£
Lighting hires	£	£	£	£
Sound hires	£	£	£	£
Other hires	£	£	£	£
Total Production costs	£	£	£	£
Salaries	£	£	£	£
Actor	£	£	£	£
Actor	£	£	£	£
Actor	£	£	£	£
Actor	£	£	£	£
Actor	£	£	£	£
Actor	£	£	£	£
Musician	£	£	£	£
Musician	£	£	£	£
Company stage manager	£	£	£	£
Total Salaries	£	£	£	£
Theatre costs	£	£	£	£
Theatre rent	£	£	£	£
Theatre contra	£	£	£	£
Fit up	£	£	£	£
Miscellaneous	£	£	£	£
Total Theatre costs	£	£	£	£
Rehearsal costs	£	£	£	£
Audition costs (casting director)	£	£	£	£
Scripts/copying	£	£	£	£

Generic expenditure budget (continued opposite).

	£	£	£	£
Rehearsal rooms	£	£	£	£
Rehearsal hires	£	£	£	£
Stage manager's petty cash	£	£	£	£
Travel	£	£	£	£
Miscellaneous	£	£	£	£
Total Rehearsal costs	£	£	£	£
Advertising and PR	£	£	£	£
Advertising	£	£	£	£
Front of house display	£	£	£	£
Print	£	£	£	£
Marketing	£	£	£	£
PR fee and expenses	£	£	£	£
Photographer and prints	£	£	£	£
Press prints	£	£	£	£
Total Advertising and PR	£	£	£	£
General Administration	£	£	£	£
Legal fees	£	£	£	£
Accountancy	£	£	£	£
Insurance	£	£	£	£
Travelling expenses	£	£	£	£
Opening night and entertaining	£	£	£	£
Administration/office costs	£	£	£	£
Total General Administration	£	£	£	£
Totals	£	£	£	£
Fees	£	£	£	£
Production	£	£	£	£
Salaries	£	£	£	£
Theatre costs	£	£	£	£
Rehearsal costs	£	£	£	£
Advertising and PR	£	£	£	£
General Administration	£	£	£	£
Total Costs	£	£	£	£
Add contingency	£	£	£	£
Costs including contingency	£	£	£	£

local town or area authority. Do they have an arts officer? If they do, then you need to go and win them over. Similarly, the local public arts funding body, if such a thing exists, will need convincing of the validity and importance of the project. Before you go and see these people, it is good to call and find out what kind of application system they have for their funds, and when the deadlines are for these applications. Even if they say that they have no funding available, they should still be able to talk to you and help you think of other sources of funding in their area. Remember that if they are at all off-hand or unhelpful, they are being paid by the government to provide this service to people just like you!

Sponsorship is a much bandied-about term that is actually very difficult to fulfil in theatre. Real sponsorship involves enormous sums of money that generate even larger sums of

The audio signal must be live before zero (0).
...nd, keep everything running until after the "quote"
post-applause, then close iris and cut audio.

(Above) The cost and possibility of borrowing equipment for mixed media shows makes a considerable difference to the budget.

(Left) Box office income will not help with issues of cash flow during a short run.

money, e.g. tennis players playing in specific shoes. For a company to consider sponsoring a theatrical event, that event has to be closely linked to what they produce or stand for, and it needs to target people that they otherwise cannot reach. For your project, financial support is much more likely to come from businesses local to the venue rather than large multi-nationals with a professed interest in the arts. It is you, as company ambassador, who needs to research these companies and convince them face to face of the value of helping. The local printers might help if you tell them that, by printing your publicity and programmes for free, they will stand to gain the customers of the theatre you are playing at, as well as of all the many marketing executives who will be coming to see your play.

The other funding option never to be underestimated is through contacts you or other members of your team might have. If someone you know is well placed in a company, can they ask for some money on your behalf? If they can, then you are much more likely to get it. People's friends or relatives might also be interested in joining a scheme that donates amounts towards the project in return for tickets to the première or some other contact to the process – many smaller amounts can add up to a great deal.

All of this demonstrates that for a producer, the conception stage is crucial both in terms of organization and of timing – the longer you have to complete this stage, whilst at the same time giving yourself an end-goal date, the easier the task will become later on.

TEAM-BUILDING AND RUNNING WORKSHOPS

At this point it is assumed that there are at least two people on board: yourself and the director. You now have to build a creative team and a production team that will back

---

Prompt Point

Almost all chapters contain ideas to use in workshop situations: see especially Chapters 1, 3 and 5.

---

your convictions and agree to embark on a project about which they know very little. It is difficult to stress just how important this part of the process is. In fact, it is probably one of the most challenging and rewarding aspects of producing.

You need to match talent with suitability for a project, availability and enthusiasm. You do not want to work with a brilliant set designer for whom your project is just a little aside and who does not want to join in. These people will need to be on hand more than for most projects and they must really want to do it – again, it is your job to convince them.

It is also your job to ensure that throughout the process they are constantly kept abreast of what is going on and that they are generally treated well, and respected by other members of the team. If you can create a conducive atmosphere, then the team will work harder and still find the job enjoyable. Simple perks like free lunches or an organized gathering for 'get to know each other' drinks are always good ways to achieve this. These perks can also be extended to the aforementioned army of casual helpers that you are gathering.

As mentioned in the previous section, running a workshop well ahead of the project – even a year or more – is a very good way to help the producer and the rest of the team assess what the show may need. The producer and the director, and any other members of the creative team that are already on board, need to sit down and decide a structure for the workshop. Do they want to make sure that

145

*Workshops help potential participants
to get to know you, and you them!*

but you will be none the wiser about your project. It is good to record on camera and video as much as possible about this process, both as a visual image for you to show to likely funders, and also to help you all remember the good things that came out of the workshops. The liberating thing about these workshops is that you need not work with a fixed team – as long as the actors are interested in pitching in with ideas and feel comfortable with the process of devising, then they should be welcome. You do need to make them aware however, that come the main project, they will not necessarily be cast. For more information and ideas on casting, see Chapters 1 and 3.

Although not really a tool for finding cast members, the workshops may still give you a new idea about something – maybe one female character would actually gain something by being played by a man, as shown by an actor in the workshop. Seeing people playing and devising often allows you to move away from type-casting and broadens your perspective on who you may need to look for in the auditioning process.

The workshop should also serve as a tester for the gut instinct. At the end of it you, as the producer, should still be convinced that this is a feasible idea – if you do not think so any more, then you will have saved a great deal of time and money by establishing this now rather than later.

PRE-PRODUCTION TASKS

Now that you have your team, you can help to orchestrate their way of working; they need to have a fair number of meetings before rehearsals begin. Since the budget is nearly always limited, the rehearsal time will also be just enough to achieve the full production. Therefore, the way to make sure that you can create the best possible project out of the material is by carefully pre-planning anything

what they have in their heads is really translatable onto the stage or do they want to see whether children will have an interest in the story? Do they want to begin to invent a style for the piece or do they want to concentrate on what amount of space and what kind of space it might need? Depending on this, the workshop design will emerge accordingly – maybe some work just with actors and other moments with a group of children or with input from designers will be required.

It is very important to start the workshops with precise goals in mind – otherwise they might end up being fun for the actors involved,

Working with children will also mean you have a guaranteed audience – their friends and family.

that will enhance or encourage the devising process.

All directors work differently. However, if you can persuade your director to think very carefully about the structure of the rehearsal time, and about what they will achieve by a certain point, then you can arrange for the rest of the team to come in to see what is happening in rehearsals. This will ensure that they have enough time to begin to do their jobs. You also need to persuade the team to divide up tasks, e.g. is there a section that is likely to be pure choreography and can the director therefore schedule in some time for the choreographer to work with the actors – similarly for the composer or dramaturg.

You also need to find out what kind of space is needed for rehearsals and what else is needed to facilitate the devising process. Once these things are established, it is your job to ensure that someone is in charge of them, e.g. the production or stage manager, or other members of the team. You and the production manager now become the motivators to all the other members of the team, to ensure that rehearsals can run as smoothly as possible and that everyone is available and present when they are needed.

As well as facilitating all of these meetings and discussions, you are now also dealing with all of the administrative aspects of the production, e.g. press releases and marketing material. This does not vary much from working on a non-devised production except

147

that you again need to persuade good press and marketing representatives (if you can afford them) to help you sell the ideas. If you have thought about it carefully in the conception stage, then this should not be a problem. If you need the input of any of the members of the team to write copy or provide images, for example, now is a good time to do this before everyone gets caught up in rehearsals. This is the stage during which the team should begin to work together very closely – if you have chosen wisely, then this should be an exciting and creative period.

The last big task before the rehearsal stage is to set up and co-ordinate auditions. There are many ways of doing this – adverts in industry magazines, talking to agents or hiring a casting director. Some of these may be less appropriate when looking for actors who will be able to work within a devising process. Often it will be better to pursue actors who have already had a good deal of experience in this field through working with other companies who devise work by contacting the companies directly. Another possibility is to ask actors to come along to a workshop and establish at that point whether they have the necessary skills. The key at this stage is to keep bringing in as many appropriate people as possible by any means available to you, to provide the widest possible choice and the most diverse influences from which you can then build a balanced and inspiring cast.

REHEARSALS AND PRODUCTION

At this stage, your job changes from being an ambassador to being a pure diplomat. By now all of your pre-planning should be paying off. Most of your jobs should be done or handed over to someone else allowing you to be in or around rehearsals as much as possible. The last thing you need to ensure is that everyone is being paid what they are owed on schedule. As well as being the moment when you begin to see the fruits of your labour, you can make yourself very useful to the rest of the team.

While the production team is busy pre-empting and scrambling together what is needed for both rehearsals and for the show itself, you can observe more closely what is going on and anticipate moments of crisis. When a new scene suddenly appears in rehearsals and everyone forgets to tell the composer or the costume designer, you might be the one to point this out. You can also continue to put gentle pressure on the director to focus on the final show, as well as creating possibilities – it is their job to get carried away and yours to keep thinking about the opening night. You also need to persuade the director and the actors to allow as many people in to see the rehearsal process, as often as possible.

The other advantage of being close to rehearsals is that you can really help the marketing and press representatives by informing them about what is happening and what might make a good story for a journalist. If the director and the actors feel confident enough after a while, you could even invite some press to come and see the work in progress, thereby giving them a better idea of what it is the audience can expect.

Apart from all of the last minute crises, which at this point should be handled by your production management team with your help if needed, you now hope that the audiences you expect will arrive and that the press and sponsors will like your show. But there is one more ingredient to help this process along, one that you will have been compiling during the rehearsal period: it is the producer's job to ensure that an informative and interesting programme for the audience to read is produced for the first night. Such a programme may give the audience extra insights into the genesis of this project and your team, providing any background information that may be needed, and be a vital place in which to thank all those funders, sponsors and loaners who have contributed to the project.

Finally, you have reached the production stage and an audience will judge whether your gut instinct was right and whether the people you gathered around you to invent the project have managed to extract a compelling and convincing piece of live performance from the initial kernel of an idea.

Checklist for the Producer

Conception and planning:
- establish who and how many people will be involved;
- decide on an approximate date for the project;
- make a decision about what venue you will be in;
- decide on your target audience;
- draw up a budget;
- put together an information pack;
- raise the funds for the project.

Team-building and running workshops:
- contact all of the prospective team members and check their availability and interest in the project;
- organize a time and a place to hold the preliminary workshop and engage performers to take part in this process.

Pre-production tasks:
- organize meetings for the entire creative team;
- implement and oversee the marketing and press strategies;
- begin to plan a structure for rehearsals;
- find a rehearsal space and all tools needed in rehearsals;
- organize auditions.

Rehearsals and production:
- organize an event to introduce the entire team before rehearsals begin;
- make sure that everyone is being paid appropriately and on time;
- keep the process moving forwards during rehearsals;
- keep abreast of all marketing and press aspects;
- organize the programme.

END NOTE
Chris Baldwin and Tina Bicât

As you have read and used this book, either by dipping into the chapters that interest you or by reading it from cover to cover, we hope that you have discovered that your initial interest in the subject of devising has deepened and perhaps become even more determined. Indeed, we hope that you will share with us the belief that the whole book, and the various voices that it represents, amounts to an affirmation of the very act of theatre in general and devising in particular.

Theatre at its best, and this includes all theatre, whether devised or otherwise, is a collaborative act requiring all those involved in its making to pool ideas and share passions. There is no place for egocentricity in the rehearsal room. But a devised piece of work can make great, memorable theatre, theatre which leaves shadows for years to come upon the memories of those lucky enough to have both made or witnessed that unrepeatable act.

Each chapter contained in this volume has drawn attention to a specific area of responsibility within the devising process and rehearsal. They have covered the excitement, energy and passion such work can generate, as well as focusing on the particular skills and contributions their specialisms make to the devising process. Some of these voices have, at times, verged on contradicting one another – something we, as editors, are not at all concerned to suffocate. Indeed, if there were not differences of opinion in a group, or at least a varying of emphases, then this group, like any other, would not be functioning dynamically. Of course internal contradictions need to be handled sensitively, honestly and with a high degree of care and respect. But a level of honest and open-hearted difference of opinion is to be expected and welcomed.

What if things do go wrong in a devising group? What if the group begins to disagree with itself to such an extent that it threatens to become delinquent to some degree or other? Or, at its most extreme – and this, in reality, rarely happens – what if the shared aim of getting a show ready for the first night becomes eclipsed by the internal tensions within the group? Like all group situations things can go wrong for a number of reasons and in a number of ways. And yet when things do go wrong they can often be traced back to decisions or procedures not having been correctly handled earlier on in the process. So while the contributors to this book have rarely addressed the issue of crisis directly, their strategies for avoiding such situations are implicit in what they have all written. So let us draw out some of these generic points.

First, all the contributors have discussed the nature of the decision-making for which they are directly responsible. They have all discussed the need for information to be given to them, or made available to them, on which they can make the correct choices according to their brief. If these contributory, yet crucial, decisions are made correctly and with all the information required, then gradually, with the help of experience, the likelihood of things going terribly wrong can usually be avoided.

The success of the devising process requires, above all, for the director and producer to be equally committed to giving their team what they need to do their jobs properly. In a devising context, neither the director nor the producer are at the top of a hierarchical power pyramid but rather at the fulcrum of a very particular process. In order to direct and produce devised theatre effectively, it is essential to find and maintain equilibrium between various oscillating lines. The team is dependent upon the director giving them a clear angle or idea for the work, but must then be supported and helped by him or her in order for them to move forward through the rehearsal process.

All contributors have discussed the importance of research at every stage of the process. Such a commitment to research is not simply to ensure that one knows as much as possible about a certain subject in order to widen the choices. By producing good quality, dependable research (and not just web pages printed out from unclear sources), the deviser, whether actor, designer, writer or stage manager, is sharing their own work with the rest of the team. Trust in you will increase if the decisions you are seen to make can be justified and explained. If your working process is amenable and substantial enough to welcome and respond to the questions of others (and, indeed, influence the decisions of others), then the act of making that critical choice will be all the more valid. Not only will the end result be stronger but also the likelihood of a crisis occurring later in the process will be dramatically reduced. People are much more likely to respond with an open mind to the creative input of others if they are sure of their own ground and are able to talk about their own ideas from an informed

perspective. As soon as company members become defensive, or treat their idea as their own property, and the group begins to divide into factions, communications fragment, and the process begins to weaken.

Implicit in everything said so far, in regard to research, is the notion of trust and communication. It is worth stating that 'trust' and 'communication' are words that have been used in this book almost more than any others except 'devising'. Trust, as anyone will tell you, cannot come out of thin air but is founded, developed and built upon bit by bit as the days and weeks go past. The better you are at both making decisions based on good research and acknowledging quickly when you have done something that might not have been right or positive, the quicker the trust will grow. From trust and good communication skills will grow a group competent in making good decisions and thus reduce the chances of things going wrong later down the path.

One point all chapters have examined explicitly is the pain of chucking out that good idea! We will all experience, if we have not already done so, that terrific sensation of a breakthrough. We have all sat in rehearsal for a few hours with a problem that just will not go away. Then suddenly you have a fantastic idea, which not only solves the problem but will give the audience the biggest surprise of their lives – the only thing is, that that one moment will mean that the costume designer will only have half of the budget she was expecting. You insist the company take the option seriously. And they do! It is agreed! Slash the costume budget and the special effect (or whatever it is) you have proposed can be purchased. But the next morning the costume designer is beside herself with grief. How can she manage on half the budget? How will her picture balance when half of it is destroyed? And so, grudgingly, the wonderful idea that seemed so exciting the day before needs to be rethought and re-balanced. It is that act of rethinking and re-balancing that will be the crucial test of company and the individual.

As all theatre companies will testify, time chases faster and faster at your heels as the first night approaches and choices have to be made and acted upon. Every department longs for more time and more money. But all devising companies will also testify that limited time and money force the discovery of some of the most exciting, memorable solutions you will ever produce and your audience will ever have the pleasure to see!

Good making!

CONTRIBUTORS

Chris Baldwin trained at Rose Bruford College of Speech and Drama. He has written and directed for many theatres across Europe including: The Nuffield Theatre, Southampton; Theatr Ochoty, Poland; Brandenburg State Theatre, Germany; Half Moon Theatre, London; Spiral Theatre Company; The Harrogate Theatre; Teatro Armar, Spain; and Teatro Sambhu, Spain. He directed Paul Barker's opera *Stone Angels* for Lontano at the Bloomsbury Theatre in London. He was Artistic Director of Proteus Touring Theatre for three years. Chris is also a playwright of more than twenty pieces of work and uses devising techniques as part of this process. He has taught directing and dramaturgy in drama schools and universities across Europe. He lives in Spain and continues to travel and direct widely.

Clive Barker's *Theatre Games* is regarded as one of the essential approaches to acting in the UK context. Trained as an actor and a member of Joan Littlewood's Theatre Workshop, he has directed widely in the UK and Europe, and as an internationally respected teacher, writer and theoretician. Clive contributes regularly to the International Workshop Festival and is joint Editor of *New Theatre Quarterly*. He is now Senior Research Fellow of Rose Bruford College.

Paul Barker is a composer of ten chamber operas, orchestral, chamber and theatre works performed and recorded internationally. He has collaborated on over twenty productions with Chris Baldwin. He is currently writing a text-book on composing for the voice. He lives in Mexico, travelling frequently as composer, pianist and conductor of his own works.

Tina Bicât's work with national, regional and fringe theatre, film, television and carnival includes productions with casts of hundreds, one-man shows, costumes devised in rehearsal, puppets, transformations, effects and conventional costume designing. Her book on *Making Stage Costumes* is published by The Crowood Press. She also works with students at St Mary's College at Strawberry Hill

Charlotte Cunningham founded Turtle Key Arts as a performance venue and production company in 1989, and has since produced and co-directed a number of theatre productions with a strong emphasis on physical theatre and devised work. She has worked with writers, choreographers, composers and designers to bring together projects for adults and children, both under the name of Turtle Key Productions and with other theatre and dance companies, and the productions have been performed both in London and internationally. Turtle Key Productions no longer runs its own venue but continues to produce theatre and dance work, and manages a large number of collaborative projects. Charlotte divides her time between production work and freelance mentoring/dramaturgy.

Bernd Keßler is deputy intendant of the Brandenburg Theatre, Germany. He trained at the Berlin High School for Theatre Directors under Manfred Wekwerth. He has directed and written plays for numerous theatres including Spiral Theatre, England, Ikeron Theatre, Berlin and the German state theatres in Frankfurt and Erfurt.

Alison King is the co-director of Turtle Key Arts, which is a performance arts company that combines production, education and training to serve theatre and dance companies, and the education sector. She trained as a stage manager and has production managed shows – from small-scale fringe to number one venues – all over England and abroad. Alison has also taught technical theatre for the last five years and has recently moved into producing, to date four children's Christmas shows and a family summer show of *The Jungle Book*.

Ruth Naylor-Smith trained in dance at the Arts Educational School, obtained a BA in Dramatic Studies from the Royal Scottish Academy of Music and Drama, and studied with Jacques Lecoq in Paris. She has been devising shows for ten years, firstly as co-artistic director of Torsion Theatre and latterly for Turtle Key Productions and Antic Hay Theatre. She is a movement director, actor and movement teacher.

Sabina Netherclift trained with Jacques Lecoq in Paris and has been devising theatre ever since. She has appeared with the Clod Ensemble (musical theatre company which devises shows featuring both actors and musicians) in *Musical Scenes 1 and 2*, *The Feast During the Plague*, *The Metamorphoses*, *The Overcoat*, *A Musical Evening* and *The Silver Swan*. Other theatre credits include *Taste* Young Vic/Space Project, *The Nativity* Young Vic, *The Suppliants*, *The Ballad of Wolves* and *Silverface* all at the Gate, *One Last Surviving* The Lyric Hammersmith and *Desire Caught by the Tail* Hong Kong Fringe Festival. She is currently working on a show inspired by the notebooks of Leonardo da Vinci.

Haibo Yu is an assistant professor in scenography at California State University Sacramento USA and has conducted worldwide design works for theatre, film and television. He obtained his first degree in Theatre Design in Beijing, China and a postgraduate degree from Central St Martin's College of Art & Design in London.

BIBLIOGRAPHY

CHAPTER 1

Barker, C., *Theatre Games* (Methuen, 1978, ISBN 0413453707)
Boal, A., *Games for Actors and Non-Actors* (Routledge, 1992, ISBN 0415061555)
Johnson, C., *House of Games* (Routledge, 1998, ISBN 087830099)
Johnstone, K., *Impro* (Theatre Art Books, 1989, ISBN 0878301178)
McKee, R., *Story* (Harper Collins, 1997, ISBN 0060391685)
Stafford Clark, M., *Letters to George* (Nick Hern Books, 1989, ISBN 1854590235)

CHAPTER 2

Hall, P. R. and Burnett, K., *Time Space* (Design Umbrella in association with the Society of British Theatre Designers, London, 1999, ISBN 0952930919)
Howard, P., *What is Scenography* (Routledge, 2001, ISBN 0415100852)
Make Space! Design for Theatre and Alternative Spaces (Design Umbrella in association with the Society of British Theatre Designers, London, 1994, ISBN 0952930900)
Reid, F., *Designing for the Theatre* (A & C Black, London, 1996, ISBN 0878300627)

CHAPTER 3

Whatever your area of interest in theatre, read as widely as you can. Everything from Stanislavsky to Martin Esslin. The following suggestions are for those actors interested in the processes of devising from different points of view (plus a very good book on looking after your voice).

Berry, C., *The Actor and the Text* (Virgin Publishing Ltd., 1993, ISBN 0863697054)
Clements, P., *The Improvised Play: the Work of Mike Leigh* (Methuen, ISBN 0413504409)
Lecoq, J., *The Moving Body* (Methuen, 2000, ISBN 0418752607)

CHAPTER 4

Aristotle/Poetics (1965) *Classical Literary Criticism* (Hill & Wang, 1989, ISBN 0809005271)
McKee, R., *Story* (1998) (Harper Collins, 1997, ISBN 0060391685)
Willett, J. (ed.), *Brecht on Theatre* (Hill & Wang, 1994, ISBN 0809005425)

CHAPTER 5

Barker, C., *Theatre Games* (Methuen, 1978, ISBN 0413453707)
Beckett, S., *Quad* (1986, ISBN 0571144861)
Brook, P., *The Empty Space* (Simon and Schuster, 1997, ISBN 0484829576)
Cage, J., *Silence* (Wesleyan University Press, 1973, ISBN 0819560286)
Wesley Balk, H., *The Complete Singer-Actor* (University of Minnesota, Minneapolis, 1985, ISBN 0816614180)

CHAPTER 6

Johnstone, K., *Impro* (Methuen, 1981, ISBN 041346430X)
Lecoq, J., *The Moving Body* (Methuen, 2000, ISBN 0413752607)

CHAPTER 7

Bicât, T., *Making Stage Costumes* (The Crowood Press, 2001, ISBN 1861264089)
Thorne, G., *Designing Stage Costumes* (The Crowood Press, 2001, ISBN 186126416X)
Waugh, N., *The Cut of Men's Clothes 1600–1900* (Theatre Art Books, 1994, ISBN 0878300252)
Waugh, N., *The Cut of Women's Clothes 1600–1930* (Theatre Art Books, 1994, ISBN 0878300260)

CHAPTER 8

Copley, S. and Killner, P., *Stage Management* (The Crowood Press, 2001, ISBN 1861264534)
Original British Theatre Directory (Richard Hare Publishing Co. Ltd., published yearly, ISBN 1870323327)
Winslow, C., *The Oberon Glossary of Theatrical Terms* (ISBN 1870259262)

CHAPTER 9

Brook, P., *The Empty Space* (Simon and Schuster, 1968, ISBN 0140135839)
Lepage, R., *Connecting Flights* (Consortium Book Sales, 1999, ISBN 1559361654)
National Guide to Funding in Arts and Culture (The Foundation Centre)
The Arts Funding Guide – The Directory of Social Change (UK)

INDEX

INDEX

INDEX